PRACTICAL
TEACHING
SKILLS
for

Other driving books from Kogan Page

The Driving Instructor's Handbook (Tenth Edition)
John Miller and Margaret Stacey
ISBN 0 7494 2135 5

Learn to Drive in 10 Easy Stages (Second Edition)
Margaret Stacey
ISBN 0 7494 0716 6

The Advanced Driver's Handbook (Second Edition)
Margaret Stacey
ISBN 0 7494 1501 0

How to Pass the Theory L Test
John Miller, Tony Scriven and Margaret Stacey
ISBN 0 7494 2279 3

SECOND EDITION

PRACTICAL TEACHING ■ SKILLS ■

for DRIVING INSTRUCTORS

JOHN MILLER ■ TONY SCRIVEN
MARGARET STACEY

KOGAN PAGE

First published in 1993
Reprinted 1994
Second Edition 1995
Reprinted 1996, 1997

Kogan Page Limited
120 Pentonville Road
London N1 9JN

© John Miller, Tony Scriven and Margaret Stacey, 1993, 1995

British Library Cataloguing in Publication Data

A CIP record for this book is available from the British Library

ISBN 0 7494 1321 2

Typeset by Paul Stringer, Rochester
Printed and bound in England by
Clays Ltd, St Ives plc

Contents

Foreword

Teaching driving requires many skills, sound theoretical knowledge of the subject and the ability to put that theory into practice in one's own driving together with tact, enthusiasm and sometimes the patience of a saint. Not many teachers have to impart a practical skill while being driven along the road at speeds of up to 70mph.

However, most important of all are the practical teaching skills needed to pass on this knowledge and ability to others. In *Practical Teaching Skills for Driving Instructors*, the authors, who between them have a wealth of experience in both driver training and driving instructor training, have put together a book that covers these skills in detail.

In a logical and sensible order, this book takes potential driving instructors and qualified ADIs who are looking to hone their knowledge through the skills required for effective driver training. It covers why people learn to drive and how they learn, communication skills and the special skills needed by driving instructors, and touches on such things as personality development and preparing for the ADI entrance exam. It also covers the ADI check test, how to prepare for it, what sort of pupil to take and a subject dear to the heart of most ADIs, how to achieve the best grading.

This book sets out in a simple and easy to understand style the many facets of training needed for an instructor to reach the required standard for the ADI examinations and contains much information that many of us would do well to revise from time to time!

John Lepine MBE,
General Manager
The Motor Schools Association of Great Britain

Preface

PRACTICAL TEACHING SKILLS for driving instructors are skills which help the instructor to 'bring about learning'.

LEARNING is the acquisition of more or less permanent changes in knowledge, understanding, skills and attitude by the learner.

TEACHING is the bringing about of these changes in the learner by creating an environment where LEARNING can take place.

The driving instructor, who has already proved that he has good knowledge and understanding, together with a sound attitude and a high level of skill, must be able to create an environment where he can transfer these attributes to his learners.

There are many books available on instructional techniques and teaching skills, but they often adopt a theoretical approach rather than a practical one.

In his foreword to *The Driving Instructor's Handbook*, Brian Austin, the ADI Registrar, states: 'The ADI that says "I have nothing further to learn – you can't teach me anything" is, quite apart from being insufferably arrogant, heading for a shock sooner or later. One of the things that one notices about a number of ADIs that consistently fail check tests is the closed minds they display. They have a method that has, in their perception, worked for years so therefore it must be perfect. On the other hand I am sure that practically all very good ADIs would admit that they are learning all the time, honing their skills: they are not too proud to learn from others'.

This book will show existing driving instructors and those wishing to become instructors how their skills can be developed in order to improve their ability to teach driving as a lifetime skill with a view to preserving life.

They will also need to be able to prepare their learner drivers for the new written theory test. To do this, instructors will have to use classroom skills, a new experience and a challenge for many of them. Teaching in the classroom has therefore been included in this book.

The book has been designed to draw together all the teaching skills necessary for good driving instruction and shows how such skills can be applied in practice. An important consideration has been the need for driving instructors to develop their teaching skills in a practical way, building on strengths and ironing out weaknesses.

Each skill is divided into its component parts and a series of checklists is provided so that you can measure how your skills are developing.

Although this book allows you to measure this improvement, it must be pointed out that there is no substitute for practical 'hands on' training with a specialist instructor training establishment or tutor, and practice and experience gained by teaching learner drivers out on the road.

When learners pass the driving test and obtain a full licence, they should see it as passing the entrance examination rather than receiving a degree. New drivers will learn much more during their first few years as drivers than they do while learning to drive and this is reflected in the high insurance premium costs imposed on them. Learning should, then, be a continuous process which lasts throughout their lives as drivers.

Similarly, when driving instructors pass their examinations and become 'approved' this is just the starting point.

Because the most effective way of learning how to teach is to teach, instructors will learn more during their first few years teaching real learners than they will on any training course!

What this book will do for you is help you to make your teaching more enjoyable and more effective, both for yourself and the learners you are teaching.

The Authors

John Miller has been involved in the driver training industry for 25 years. He is an Approved Driving Instructor and an HGV Class 1 instructor. John runs a driving school in West Sussex for learner drivers, motorcyclists and commercial vehicle drivers. The school also operates a driving instructor training centre.

Tony Scriven has been an Approved Driving Instructor since 1972, specialising in the training and retraining of driving instructors from a training centre in Leeds. He is a Fellow of the Institute of Sales and Marketing Management and a Member of the Institute of Training and Development. Tony has written numerous articles on driving instruction in the trade papers and has lectured on a variety of subjects at ADI seminars and conferences. He is responsible for all the illustrations in this book.

Margaret Stacey has also been an Approved Driving Instructor since 1972. Margaret has written various books on driving instruction and operates an instructor training establishment in Derbyshire. She also markets an Instructor Home Study Programme which is widely used by those preparing for the Part 1 - Written Examination and is incorporated into the training schemes of many training establishments throughout the UK.

John Miller and Margaret Stacey will already be known to most driving instructors as the co-authors of *The Driving Instructor's Handbook* (also published by Kogan Page) which is a reference manual for driving instructors and is included in the material which the Driving Standards Agency recommend all potential ADIs to read when preparing for the entrance examinations.

The authors have received a large number of requests, both from ADIs and those training to become approved, for a practical training manual to complement the *Driving Instructor's Handbook*.

Practical Teaching Skills for Driving Instructors has been produced to fulfil that need by showing instructors how to apply the theory contained in the Handbook in a practical way.

All three authors are expert practitioners of skills training, ADI National Joint Council Tutors and Members of the Institute of Master Tutors of Driving, and the content of this book has come largely from their experience in training people to become Department of Transport Approved Driving Instructors.

A central part of the training courses designed by the authors has been to develop the instructor characteristics, instructional techniques and practical teaching skills of their trainees.

This book will enable both existing and prospective driving instructors to benefit from that experience.

Much of the information in the book is based on established principles for the implementation of practical teaching skills drawing on what is 'common knowledge'. The authors acknowledge that much of what is written is not new, but what is unique is the drawing together of all the practical teaching skills required by driving instructors into one book and presenting the content in a practical manner.

It must be stressed that there is no substitute for practical training and experience and this book forms the basis of specialised training courses for prospective and existing driving instructors and proprietors of ADI training establishments and their trainers.

For information on specialist training, please contact:

John Miller	Tony Scriven	Margaret Stacey
57 North Street	35–41 New Briggate	The Mount
Chichester	Leeds	53 Heanor Road
West Sussex	West Yorkshire	Ilkeston
PO19 1NB	LS2 8JD	Derbyshire
		DE7 8DY
Tel 01243 783540	*Tel* 0113 294 1456	*Tel* 0115 932 4499

Acknowledgements

The authors wish to acknowledge all the dedicated, hard-working men and women who spend their time in all weathers trying to convince the general public of the need for professional driving instruction, more lessons and extra practice.

We acknowledge the help and assistance given by the Driving Standards Agency, particularly with reference to the reproduction of DSA assessment and marking sheets. It should be borne in mind that these forms are under constant review.

For the information and advice given on teaching deaf people how to drive, we are indebted to Mrs Elwyn Reed MBE.

We are grateful for constructive suggestions for improving this book from Brian Austin, the ADI Registrar; Brian Cattle MA, BEd, DipEE, CEng, the DSA's Educational Consultant; and numerous Supervising Examiners (ADI). Where possible these suggestions have been incorporated.

We also acknowledge that, when teaching people how to drive, both men and women are equally as effective. Therefore, in order to avoid sexual stereotyping in this book, the term 'he' will equally apply to 'she' and vice versa. This stems from a desire to avoid ugly and cumbersome language, and no discrimination, prejudice or bias is intended.

How to Use This Book

Once in a while a new book appears which can change the way in which we look at a familiar subject.

The subject of this book is 'driving instruction'. The book is the first on the subject which provides you with all the information you need to be an effective teacher of driving, while simultaneously offering you an ongoing programme of self-development.

The vast majority of readers of this book will fall into one of the following three categories:

- those wishing to become driving instructors;
- those who are already driving instructors but want to improve their skills;
- those who train driving instructors.

The way in which you will need to use this book is likely to vary depending on which of the above three categories of reader you fall into.

You may read the book from cover to cover, or use it to check up on the many specialist skills which you will need to use every day whilst carrying out your training duties.

The chapter headings and sub-headings will give an overview of what the book is all about and how it is structured. Start by reading through these chapter headings, making a note of any which you think will be of immediate interest to you.

There is a more detailed index at the end of the book. The book can thus be used as a reference source and 'dipped into' using the index whenever you need information on a particular topic.

Remember, you cannot learn a new technique or improve on an existing one just by reading about it. You have to practise what you have learnt from the book with your learners or trainees and continually evaluate how successful you have been.

1

Introducing Practical Teaching Skills for Driving Instructors

PRACTICAL TEACHING SKILLS (PTS) for driving instructors are not new. Many Approved Driving Instructors have been using them for years without even realising what they were called. It is probable that, when becoming driving instructors, they brought with them practical teaching skills remembered from school, gained through previous jobs, from the armed services or through other experience, for example as a parent.

These practical skills and techniques which have been transferred from previous environments are known by educationalists as 'transferable personal skills'. This term is used to define skills personal to the individual which can be used in many different situations.

For example, a pedestrian who is about to cross a busy main road uses skills in judging the speed and distance of oncoming traffic. These skills when recognised and 'transferred' to the new environment of driving become very useful when waiting to turn right across oncoming traffic. The skills are the same, but the environment is different.

Before the term 'transferable personal skills' was introduced, such skills were known as communication skills, interpersonal skills, or social skills.

When teaching learner drivers to cope with the fast, complicated, potentially dangerous and ever-changing environment in which motor vehicles are driven, it is vital that driving instructors develop their transferable personal skills and PTS in order to be able to ensure that learning takes place.

Remember, that driving instructors are the only teachers whose 'desk' is travelling down the high street at 30 miles per hour and the safety of themselves, their pupils and other road users is dependent on their control and effectiveness.

To survive in what is becoming an increasingly competitive market-place, both new and existing Approved Driving Instructors need to work continually at improving their PTS, instructor characteristics and fault assessment, as well as developing their business expertise.

The driving instruction industry has regrettably not yet been able to come up with qualifications which compare with the National Vocational Qualifications (NVQs) now commonly available in other industries. NVQs are designed to recognise and build on 'competences' or things that trainees or learners have proved they can do. Training for NVQs relies heavily on the practical side rather than the theoretical.

This book is designed to improve the PTS of driving instructors, rather than to equip them to debate the subject in an abstract setting.

As a professional driving instructor you need to be able to persuade your learners to do whatever you wish them to do, in the way that you want them to do it. Most of the PTS dealt with in this book are dependent on effective communication skills. The instructor who can communicate effectively is far more likely to succeed in transferring his own knowledge, understanding, skills and attitude to the learner.

Driving a motor car is potentially the most dangerous thing that people are likely to do in their lifetimes. Knowledge of the *Highway Code* and the ability to drive with a high degree of expertise are not in themselves sufficient qualities to be able to teach somebody else how to drive. The number of parents and spouses who have been unsuccessful in teaching their loved ones bears witness to this fact.

Department of Transport Approved Driving Instructors (ADIs) should aim to teach all their pupils 'SAFE DRIVING FOR LIFE'.

In order to qualify, those wishing to become ADIs are required to demonstrate not only their knowledge and driving ability, but also their communication skills and instructional techniques.

This book concentrates on showing potential and existing ADIs how to improve their teaching and communication skills so that they are better equipped to teach others safe driving for life. It also covers the preparation required for all three parts of the ADI qualifying examination.

PTS can be developed to help you interact with your pupils, building on existing transferable skills. Many of these skills are not only 'transferable' from one environment to another but are also 'transferable' from the instructor to the pupil.

To be a successful driving instructor relies not only on the traditional interpersonal, communication and social skills but also on being able to:

- use and interpret body language;
- sell ideas and concepts;
- solve problems;
- assess faults; and
- make immediate decisions with safety in mind.

To become qualified as an ADI, as well as the foregoing qualities, one also requires learning and study skills, and a basic understanding of role play.

ADIs are required to be able to communicate with their pupils in a variety of ways to suit the perceived needs of each individual pupil. They are involved with selling, whether it be 'selling' themselves or their services to potential pupils or selling ideas and concepts to existing pupils.

All of these skills have been included in this book because they are the core skills which ADIs must master in order to be able to develop their careers. It is the ability to pass on many of these same skills to their pupils that makes them effective as teachers. This book shows instructors how to improve their effectiveness as teachers by developing these PTS.

As we have already said, PTS and the other transferable personal skills are not developed overnight. The ADI who wishes to develop should consider training and retraining as well as continually monitoring his performance and effectiveness. The necessity to practice these skills while giving driving lessons is just as vital to the ADI's development, as practice is to his pupil. To be able to learn from each encounter with a new pupil and structure a self-development programme the ADI must be aware how studying, learning and teaching can all be made more effective.

Even more important is the ability of the ADI to continually develop his own transferable personal skills and assist his pupils in doing the same. As well as driving ability, the skills of decision making, prioritising and problem solving are just as important to the learner and qualified driver as they are to the instructor.

1.1

WHY ARE PRACTICAL TEACHING SKILLS SO IMPORTANT?

To drive safely on today's crowded roads requires knowledge, understanding, skill and an attitude that not only shows courtesy and consideration for other road users but also the ability to make allowances for the mistakes of others – a 'defensive attitude'.

The development of sound PTS detailed in this book will assist you in achieving the objective of teaching driving as a lifetime skill. Many of the skills outlined are just as important to the development of the learner as they are to the development of the instructor. They are 'transferable' from one to the other.

It is a bit like preparing for the ADI Part 2 (own driving) examination.

> *The first person you have to teach how to drive is yourself. If you cannot get your own driving up to the required standard, then how can you possibly expect to teach others how to drive properly?*

The same principle applies to the skills other than driving. If you cannot master the skills of risk assessment, problem solving and decision making yourself, how can you expect to teach your pupils how to master them?

The demand for individuals to master a wide range of skills has come from employers, educational and validating bodies, the National Council for Vocational Qualifications and from government via the Training Agency.

With regard to raising the standard of driving and driving instruction skills, the Driving Standards Agency has introduced a recommended syllabus for learner drivers which should be taught by all ADIs.

Regrettably, with the performance criteria-based testing system which has evolved in this country, and the limited amount of time and money which the general public sees as being suitable when they are learning to drive, ADIs are encouraged to teach people how to pass a test instead of teaching them how to drive safely for life.

For similar reasons, the same applies to the ADI qualifying examinations – candidates are often trained only to 'pass the test'. The PTS outlined in this book will equip instructors and ADI trainers to teach skills for life, but the onus of responsibility to do this lies with the instructor.

The Driving Standards Agency's (DSA) check test system which has been intensified during the past few years, has shown many existing ADIs to be inarticulate or tongue-tied, lacking in initiative and unable to provide for their pupils an environment in which learning took place. Many were also found to be reluctant to accept criticism. Others were unable to identify faults committed by their pupils, some of which were repetitive or even serious in nature.

In addition to the clear external justification for all ADIs to develop their skills there is the individual benefit of personal development and the satisfaction which goes with it.

The techniques of self-evaluation and analysing and judging your own abilities and their development will inevitably result in your getting to know yourself better. You will then be better able to plan your career development.

Economic pressures also demand an improvement in the teaching skills of driving instructors. In today's economic climate competition is strong, so those ADIs who can demonstrate more effective skills than their competitors are more likely to survive.

The self-evaluation process will also enable you to identify characteristics which might hinder your interrelationships with other people and show you how to modify them, making you more personable in the process.

1.2

WHO SHOULD DEVELOP PRACTICAL TEACHING SKILLS?

- The skills covered in the book are highly transferable and will be of value to all ADIs who are concerned with improving their own interpersonal effectiveness, or the skills of their learners.

- Existing ADIs who wish to improve their career prospects will benefit from enhancing and developing their PTS.

- ADIs who will need to prepare learner drivers for the new Theory Test.

- Those seeking employment will have much to gain by being able to offer these abilities to prospective employers and those already in employment or self-employed will gain by building on their existing strengths and overcoming their weaknesses.

- Those who simply want to become more self-confident or wish to be able to influence their peers more effectively will gain by following the guidelines provided in this book.

- ADIs preparing for their periodic Test of Continued Ability and Fitness (check test) will find improved communication skills and PTS will give them greater confidence, and a better chance of achieving a higher grade.

- Trainee driving instructors will find that a better understanding of the skills required when teaching people how to drive will stand them in good stead when taking the ADI qualifying examinations, particularly Part 1 (written examination) and Part 3 (instructional ability examination). It must be reiterated that there is no substitute for practical hands-on training and practice. You cannot learn how to drive from a book and neither can you learn how to teach somebody how to drive from a book. The best way to learn how to teach is to teach!

- For tutors of driving instructors or staff instructors at instructor training establishments, developing the skills contained in this book is extremely pertinent and totally compatible with the criteria for approval under the Approved Driving Instructor Training Establishments (ADITE) or Driving Instructors' Association Recommended Training Establishments (DIARTE) schemes.

1.3

HOW ARE PRACTICAL TEACHING SKILLS DEVELOPED?

The development of PTS is an arduous, continuous and lifelong process, with each new encounter offering you the opportunity to improve your skills. Learning occurs in a variety of different ways but, as in most things, a systematic approach is invariably more effective than one that is haphazard.

Trial and error in using skills will give some insight into the ones which are the most effective in different situations and with different pupils. Reflection on your successes and failures will also assist you in developing your PTS.

Formal training and structured learning, both in the classroom and out on the road, will be invaluable to instructors wishing to develop their own skills. This would apply even more when developing the more active learning strategies such as role playing exercises and fault assessment skills. Formal training would allow you to practice new skills in a safe and controlled setting before trying them out on real learner drivers or trainees in the real world.

Experience gained while watching demonstrations given by your tutor will be invaluable when you have to demonstrate skills to your pupils. Training should be a chain of learning which never ends. Trainees will learn from their tutors; learners will learn from their driving instructors; instructors will learn from their pupils; and, in turn, this information will get fed back to the tutor via the instructor and passed on down to other instructors.

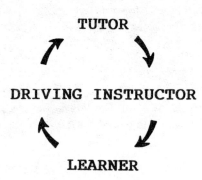

TUTOR

DRIVING INSTRUCTOR

LEARNER

Chain of learning

In helping you to develop your PTS, this book will act as a permanent source of reference and allow you to analyse and review the constituent components of the various skills and monitor how well you are using them.

The challenge for you is to adopt a frame of mind which welcomes each learning strategy, particularly those which require a more active approach.

> *The key element in teaching others how to drive (and in learning to drive) is* PRACTICE.

When teaching your pupils how to drive, every opportunity must be taken by you to practice the skills contained in this book.

Some of the skill training in the book can be threatening to both learners and instructors alike. If care is not taken, embarrassment and offence can be caused when analysing people's behaviour. Because of this, teaching has to be delivered in a sensitive way.

You should appreciate this fact from the outset. If you adopt too strict an approach, then your learners are unlikely to enjoy the experience and may feel reluctant to participate. Sensitivity must be shown to all your learners and is itself a transferable personal skill.

Always remember that criticism can be very demotivating. Encouragement when needed, and praise when deserved, will bring about more improvement than all the criticism in the world.

Chapter 2 explains how people learn. As a learner of PTS and transferable personal skills yourself, you must accept that training will not be easy and will demand a high degree of self-motivation and discipline. This is all part of your own learning process and will give you a better understanding of how your own learners may feel when they are struggling to master new skills.

You will have to learn how to evaluate your own strengths and weaknesses and will perhaps see yourself for the first time in your life as others see you. This is also part of the learning process.

> *It is only when you see yourself as other people do that you can start to modify your own behaviour so that more effective personal relationships and skills can be established.*

Never forget that there is no such thing as a bad learner, although some learners do find it more difficult to pick things up than others.

The skill of the teacher is in knowing when to encourage, praise, question, explain, demonstrate, repeat and assess to bring out the best in the pupil, thereby ensuring that learning may take place. Just as your learners need to learn from any mistakes they make during a driving lesson, you need to learn from your own instructional errors.

At the end of every lesson, you should ask yourself:

- Has learning taken place?
- Is there anything more that I could have done to assist my pupil in achieving the objectives set?

Only by continually evaluating your own performance in this way will you be able to improve and develop your PTS.

By using this book in a practical manner, you can learn how to improve your PTS. This will benefit your pupils and help you to achieve the highest possible grading on your Check Test.

If you are not happy with the grading you achieved on your last Check Test, you might consider either telephoning or making an appointment to see your SE(ADI).

This will enable the SE to give you guidance on any particular aspects of your teaching which may not be up to standard. Listen carefully to any advice given and study carefully the sections in this book which relate to it. You should then be able to understand more clearly what you should be doing in the car, and compare this with what you have been doing. Remember that learning is a continuous process!

2

Why People Learn to Drive and How They Learn

Before setting out to improve your Practical Teaching Skills (PTS), it will be useful for you to understand why people learn to drive, what motivates them to learn, how learning takes place and what barriers to learning exist.

2.1

THE BENEFITS OF LEARNING TO DRIVE

People learn to drive for a variety of reasons, but it is doubtful whether they ever fully realise the benefits to be gained until they have passed the driving test and become mobile. Think of your friends who drive and try to imagine how drastically their lives would change if they were to lose their licence.

When your pupils begin learning to drive they may be doing so for any of the following reasons:

- social, domestic or leisure pursuits;
- business and employment reasons;
- personal satisfaction;
- the need for independent mobility.

Other learners may be trying to rebuild their confidence after an illness or perhaps the death of a loved one; some may have time on their hands and think that learning to drive seems like a good idea while others may wish to learn merely because most of their friends can drive.

Whatever their reasons, it is only after they have passed the test that your pupils will realise how the other benefits gained from being able to drive will improve their quality of life.

The main benefits are:

- greater freedom and mobility;
- improved confidence and status;
- better employment or promotion potential;
- increased earning power.

When you consider these benefits, driving lessons should be seen as remarkably good value for money. When selling lessons, outlining these benefits to your pupils can be a very effective way of justifying what you charge.

It can be very useful to know why pupils wish to learn to drive as it will enable you to use those reasons for motivational support.

For example, if the pupil is finding a particular manoeuvre difficult, or complains about how much the lessons are costing, you should be able to placate them by saying, for instance, 'think how much easier it is going to be for you to get the kids to school each day!'.

Because of the cost involved in learning to drive, it is unusual to find learners who are not motivated to some degree. However, they do exist. For example, a husband who has lost his licence through drinking and driving may want his wife to learn so that he doesn't lose his social life. The wife may have no interest in driving at all and may therefore find it difficult to learn. Stressing the benefits mentioned previously may help overcome this lack of motivation.

2.2

MOTIVATION FOR LEARNING TO DRIVE

MOTIVATION in learning to drive embodies *all* of the factors, both internal and external, which help pupils to attain their goal.

Modern thinking holds that the strongest motivator is the need within people to fulfil the ambitions on which they have set their minds. Quite often the need for achievement will be linked to money or prestige.

If you understand some of the internal factors governing motivation, it should greatly assist you in structuring your lessons to develop the external factors which motivate each particular pupil.

Adults are most strongly motivated by the practical application of new knowledge or skills, and will often be more concerned with passing the test than in acquiring an understanding which will equip them for a lifetime of safe driving. In order to achieve the latter, therefore, any theoretical content needs to be linked not only to the driving test but also to the skills and understanding required to achieve the longer term aim.

2.3

HOW ADULTS LEARN

Learning can be described as nature's way of enabling us to adapt and survive in a fast-moving and complicated environment. The driving environment is faster and more complicated than most: problem solving and decision making often have to be carried out without the time – which is available in most other environments – to think things through.

Often, safety is in question. Poor assessment of a situation and a wrong decision could be disastrous not only for the decision maker but for any passengers or other road-users present.

Teaching can be described as creating an environment in which learning takes place. As a professional instructor, your car is your classroom.

The professional driving instructor must accept four assumptions:

- Learning is a good thing because it enriches people's lives.
- While learning is inevitable and takes place all the time, the quantity and quality of learning can be massively increased if it is done deliberately rather than left to chance.
- Learning is continuous – therefore, it makes sense for it never to cease.
- Shared learning is much easier to sustain than solo learning.

You could give someone the keys to a vehicle parked in the middle of a field and say, 'Teach yourself how to drive that car. I will be back in two hours to see how you are getting on.' Surprisingly, if you came back two hours later, that person would have gained by his own initiative some basic ability in driving. Of course, we are not suggesting that you adopt this method.

Learning is the acquiring, over time, of skills, knowledge, understanding and attitudes. Learning is changing your behaviour so that you are able to do something which you couldn't do before.

Gender, race, age and intelligence have only indirect effects on a person's ability to learn. Recent research suggests that males and females use different parts of their brain in different ways to arrive at the same answers to similar questions. In view of a fall in the number of under 25-year-olds and an increase in the number of people in the 25–54 age group, it is likely that a greater proportion of older people will present themselves for driving lessons. Their training needs will probably vary from those of younger people.

Individuals' characters and family backgrounds are more likely to influence the way in which they learn than their age or gender alone.

> *In a structured learning programme, such as a course of driving lessons, both the pupil and the instructor should be able to see and measure any change in behaviour. This should allow both parties to decide how successfully learning has taken place.*

Learning takes place in a sequence involving three interrelated stages. This is known as *the learning circle*.

```
        Learning knowledge, attitudes
                  skills
```

```
                                  Practising new skills
                                  using knowledge and
                                           attitudes
```

```
Reflecting on new behaviour,
skills  used, and modifying
attitude when necessary
```

The Learning Circle

Adults learn mainly through their senses, which provide them with information about the environment in which they live. These senses are personal to the individual and any two learners receiving the same information from their senses in a given situation, may PERCEIVE things differently. For example, one learner driver approaching a 'meeting' situation, might perceive it as being potentially dangerous and decide to hold back. Another learner approaching a similar situation, might perceive no danger at all and go charging through the closing gap.

From the beginning, you should be aware that no two pupils are likely to react to a given situation in the same way. One of the golden rules of teaching is NEVER ASSUME.

Remember that in order to be able to teach a person how to drive, firstly you have to know all about driving, secondly you have to know all about that person!

In learning to drive the three main senses used are sight, hearing and touch. However, other senses are sometimes used. For example, the sense of smell could make the driver aware that the engine is over-heating or something is burning.

THE IMPORTANCE OF SIGHT

In the learning process, sight is the most important of the senses. When teaching others to drive you can use this sense in a number of ways to improve the quality of the learning taking place.

> *Whether it be by giving a demonstration, drawing the learner's attention to actual situations ahead, or by using visual aids while giving an explanation, teaching which is comprehended through the sense of sight will be most effective in fixing things in the minds of learners.*

There is an old saying in teaching: 'I hear – I forget; I see – I remember; I do – I understand'. The truth in this makes it possible to teach a blind person how to control a car – one of the authors of this book, John Miller, has actually done so – although the practice would, of course, need to be in controlled situations with the instructor telling the driver when to go and when to stop etc. However, because of the lack of sight, a blind person would never be allowed to drive on the road!

The following diagram shows the proportions in which our senses gather information – our use of the diagram in this book itself testifies to the effectiveness of sight in the learning process.

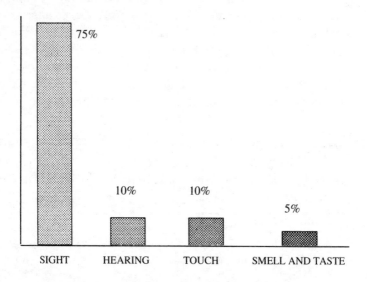

The proportions in which our senses gather information

If you told three learners in a classroom that 75 per cent of learning takes place through sight, with only 10 per cent occurring through touch, each of the students may have his own idea of what 75 per cent looks like in relation to 10 per cent. By showing the visual aid, each pupil is able to picture the different proportions, thereby achieving a uniformity of perception which matches that of the students to that of the teacher.

The ability to persuade pupils to see and perceive things as the teacher does is a vital ingredient when teaching people how to drive.

As well as sight, hearing and touch play an important part and you need to ensure that when seeing situations, hearing the noise of the engine, and feeling the clutch coming to biting point, the learner not only develops all three senses but also the awareness and perception which go with them.

AWARENESS

In driving, awareness involves not only the perception and interpretation of one's own vehicle speed, position and direction of travel, but also the recognition of other hazards in time to take the necessary safe action.

Perception and awareness are the first steps towards performing a skill such as driving. Awareness is dependent on the interpretation and meaning the brain attaches to the information it receives from the senses. This involves not only looking with the eyes but also using the mind and calling upon existing knowledge from previous experience to 'see' with the mind. What is actually seen with the eyes is not always the same as what is perceived by the brain.

Optical illusions offer evidence of this. They may be caused by distortion through perspective or by a lack of intermediate visual keys which help the viewer to gauge distance accurately.

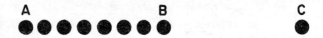

THE DISTANCE between A and B appears to be longer than that between B and C. The illusion occurs because the space between A and B is measured out in evenly spaced dots, filling the area for the eye. The distance between B and C can only be guessed at because there are no intermediate points.

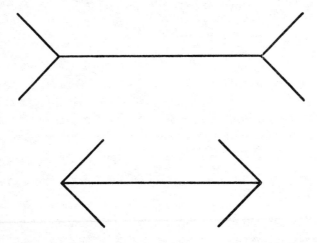

THE LENGTHS of the two horizontal lines appear unequal because of the directional arrows at the ends. Where the arrows branch outward, the line seems to be stretched out beyond its actual length. Where they branch in, the line seems to be strictly enclosed and shortened. Both of the lines are exactly the same length.

This visual distortion, plus a weakness in the driver's ability to judge correctly the width of the vehicle being driven, or that of approaching vehicles, can have very serious consequences.

What each student actually perceives while learning not only depends on the individuality of his senses but on how that particular person has learnt to see and interpret things. You may need to modify the student's perception to make it compatible with your own as an expert on the subject.

Incoming sensations are instantly compared with existing knowledge stored in the memory from previous experiences. The compatibility of these memories can either help or hinder learning of any new material. Where the new information is compatible with existing knowledge and thoughts, the established memories will be reinforced. For example, somebody learning to play tennis who is already a good squash player may find the learning less difficult because both sports are very similar. This is called POSITIVE TRANSFER OF LEARNING.

Sometimes previous knowledge can be a hindrance to learning. An example of this could be someone who decides to learn to drive a car and has been used to riding a motorcycle in scrambling trials, an activity where success is dependent on the frequent taking of risks. Put this rider behind the wheel of a car on the road and the difference in the steering, the width and length of the vehicle and the differing speed norms required may all hinder the learning process. This is called NEGATIVE TRANSFER.

In this particular case, the learner is likely to be going for gaps which are too narrow, approaching hazards much too fast and struggling to master the steering at the same time.

TRANSFER OF LEARNING can also take place. This happens when a pupil uses skills which have been learnt in other environments to help in learning to drive. Examples include problem solving, decision making and prioritising, all of which form a part of everyday life in today's society. You will often be able to relate or transfer your pupil's existing skills to help in driving. However, where the new information is not compatible with established knowledge, it may be totally rejected.

It will take time for learners to establish the many thousands of memory connections needed to be able to drive safely, along with patience and understanding on your part. What you should try to do is make sure that the pupil 'sees' situations in the same way that you see them.

Other basic requirements which are necessary for learning to take place are:

PERCEPTION,
ATTENTION,
ACTIVITY, and
INVOLVEMENT.

THE IMPORTANCE OF PERCEPTION

The senses vary from pupil to pupil and so does their perception. You will need to make your pupil's perception reasonably compatible with your own.

When you are driving along a wet road you will think that you 'see' a three-dimensional scene of slippery tarmac. What you *actually* see (the image in the eye) is neither slippery nor three-dimensional. This can only mean that you create in your mind a 'model' of what is there. You see the road as being 'wet' or 'slippery' because of the previous experience of such things you have 'fixed' in your mind.

A good example of this would be the lights of an oncoming vehicle on a dark country road at night. The amount of sensory information is very limited indeed but with your experience you should not have a problem with interpreting it. You cannot see the vehicle but you know that it is there! You will build an image of the type and size of vehicle to which the lights belong and decide whether any defensive action is required.

Drawing on your own experience, you will need to help your pupils to 'fix' such things in their minds. This can be done by using question and answer routines regarding road surface, weather conditions etc.

The diagram below gives an illustration of how the mind sometimes 'sees' things which may not be there in reality.

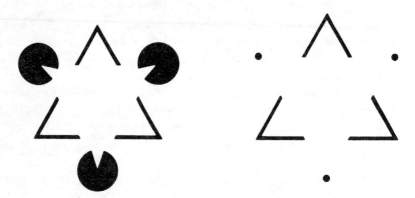

Kanizsa figures (from **Synopleveda Figures***, S. Rubin, 1915)*

The central triangle in each of the figures is an illusion. Although we see the edges as sharp and clear, they are not there. There is no actual brightness difference across the edges; the triangle must therefore be constructed in the mind of the observer.

In the early stages of learning to drive some pupils will have difficulty in judging the width and length of the car they are driving, and the speed, distance and size of oncoming traffic.

At night the problem for the inexperienced driver may be made worse by an optical illusion called IRRADIATION. This is a physiological phenomenon that occurs when the eye focuses on neighbouring bright and dark areas.

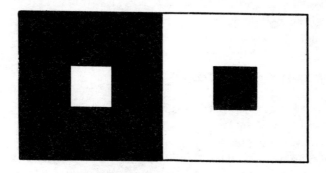

Optical illusion caused by irradiation

Although both square-within-square patterns are identical in size, the image of the dark area always tends to encroach upon that of the bright, making the small black square appear larger than the small white one.

Because illusions of this nature could have dangerous repercussions for your pupils, you should encourage them to take lessons at night so that you are there to give guidance and can help to resolve any problems which may occur.

Perception is not always under the complete control of the learner and occasionally the mind will wander off in an unrelated direction.

ATTENTION

It is often difficult to maintain pupils' attention without a break or change of activity. For this reason, most lessons in schools are of 50 minutes' duration only. Those instructors conducting intensive courses should take account of the concentration levels of each individual student and plan for changes of activity, coffee breaks etc in order not to OVERLOAD the learner.

> *If you do not have the attention of your pupil, learning is unlikely to take place.*

You should watch for non-verbal signals from the pupil which may indicate boredom, impatience or fatigue (see section 3.6 – Body Language).

ACTIVITY AND INVOLVEMENT

One of the ways of helping to keep pupils attentive is to actively involve them in the learning experience. Try to avoid very long briefings or explanations with no periods of physical involvement.

Activity, however, should not only be thought of as physical. Learning to drive obviously involves a lot of physical activity but it is often the mental involvement which initiates the physical response to a situation. The more active and involved the novice is in the learning experience, the more he or she will normally remember. This is why PUPIL CENTRED LEARNING is so vital when teaching someone how to drive. The good instructor will help learners to think and reason things out for themselves, leading them to the desired conclusion.

Although you can use questions to test a pupil's understanding of what he should be doing and why it is important, it is through physically carrying out the task that most learning will take place. This 'doing' VALIDATES the teaching.

Traditionally, there are three different instructional styles commonly used by driving instructors. These are known as:

- the Didactic,
- the Socratic, and
- the Facilitative methods.

Depending on the individual student's needs, subject matter and context, the good instructor will use a mixture of these styles as the situation demands.

The Didactic Method   This method allows the passing on of information or facts with little intellectual activity on the part of the learner. Typical examples of this style of instruction are:

- teaching the answers to questions without confirming the pupil's understanding of the reasoning behind them; or
- telling the pupil to 'Always look round before moving off' without explaining why or finding out if the pupil knows what he or she is looking for.

Although this instructional style is limited it can be useful, provided learners make use of the knowledge gained during their driving practice.

The Socratic Method   This method derives from an early form of 'questioning' practised by a Greek philosopher and refined by Socrates. A series of step-by-step questions is asked which are designed to lead the learner towards the solution of a problem or statement of principle.

Open-ended or pointed questions which encourage active and creative participation, insight and contemplation, will bring about better understanding by the pupil than closed questions which only require a 'Yes' or 'No' response. For example, when teaching a learner how to turn right you might ask:

'What is the first thing you would do before turning right?'
'Well, I would give a signal.'
'Wouldn't you do anything before that?'
'Oh yes, I would check my mirror.'
'Why is that important?'
'Well, I suppose there could be a motorcyclist overtaking me.'
'That's correct. And what would he be likely to do if you suddenly put on your signal as he was about to overtake you?'
'Well, he might suddenly brake or swerve around me.'
'Yes – so you would have caused him inconvenience or possible danger, wouldn't you?'
'Yes, I suppose so.'
'That's good. So, now you know why the "Mirror–Signal –Manoeuvre" routine is so important don't you?

Because these open-ended questions are so important they are dealt with in more detail in Section 3.2.

Letting the learner explain correct procedures to you, the teacher, can be a very effective way of bringing about learning.

The Facilitative Method This is more 'PUPIL-CENTRED' than 'INSTRUCTOR-CENTRED' because it involves a higher level of participation from your learners, with them having to accept more responsibility for their learning.

Some aspects of driving instruction lend themselves to this 'pupil-centred' approach. For example:

- learning the rules in the *Highway Code*;
- learning about basic car maintenance from a book; or
- memorising basic driving procedures such as MSM, PSL or LAD.

Pupil-centred activities are quite useful when teaching in small groups where the instructor should act as a catalyst by:

- providing the necessary resources; and
- setting tasks for the learners to involve themselves in.

All knowledge gained through such activities must be transferable to driving practice. You will need to check that your pupils fully understand all the safety implications of practically applying the knowledge they have gained. This will also apply to the setting of homework and in-between lesson tasks which will need to be validated during practical sessions.

2.4

LEARNING WITH FRIENDS AND RELATIVES

Although many people still learn to drive with friends or relatives it has been estimated that probably 95 per cent of all learners taking the Driving Test have had some professional instruction.

It may be that they have their initial instruction with a professional in order to acquire the basic skills required to control the vehicle or, more commonly, they acquire the basic skills with a friend or relative and then come to the professional just before the 'L' test saying 'I just want to make sure I'm doing everything right!'.

Of course, in the latter case it is rather like 'shutting the stable door after the horse has bolted'. It is in this sort of situation that you will have a selling job to do. This may be in the form of selling more lessons, if there is enough time and money available, or selling the idea of postponing the test in order to give the pupil more time to improve and practice the correct procedures.

Unless the friend or relative carrying out the teaching has some form of instructional background, and is a reasonably good driver, it is a distinct disadvantage if the learner has received no lessons at all from a professional instructor.

Most friends or relatives tend to use trial and error methods, and the whole process can end up becoming unpleasant for both learner and teacher. It is also common for the person teaching to be out of date on traffic law, driving techniques and the requirements of the 'L' test. As in most training, a structured approach is usually much more effective in helping the learners to achieve their objectives.

2.5

STRUCTURED TRAINING AND PRACTICE

The benefits of learning with a professional instructor should be:

- a better rapport between teacher and pupil;
- a saving in time and trouble;
- a higher level of knowledge, understanding, attitude and skill; and
- a better chance of passing the 'L' test and accomplishing safe driving for life.

To achieve the above objectives the professional driving instructor needs an understanding of how adults learn. Only through this understanding will the instructor be able to structure a programme of learning to suit the individual needs of each pupil (see section 4.1 – Teaching by Objectives).

One of the most effective methods of instruction would be to use educational or instructional BEHAVIOURAL OBJECTIVES. Although there are no hard and fast rules, the educational psychologist Bloom has identified three main categories of learning which are likely to be used as a basis for deciding the mode of instruction. As outlined in

Taxonomy of Educational Objectives: Handbook 1 (David McKay, New York, 1956), these are:

- COGNITIVE DOMAIN;
- AFFECTIVE DOMAIN; and
- PSYCHOMOTOR DOMAIN.

Cognitive domain (knowing or thinking) – Behavioural objectives relating to the cognitive domain are concerned with information and knowledge. Cognition is the name given to the mental processes – such as sensation, perception and thinking – by which knowledge may be apprehended. By classifying levels of cognition, Bloom provided a guideline by which the degree of complexity of thought involved in performing a task may be reflected in the construction of learning objectives.

Cognitive domain learning will usually be taught using conventional lessons and formally planned instruction.

Affective domain (feeling or valuing) – This relates to the feelings, attitudes, emotions and values of the trainee. The following sequence shows the usual development of affective characteristics:

1. Learner/trainee becomes aware of feelings about a particular event/activity/topic.
2. Learner/trainee conforms to instructions given by instructor/trainer regarding how he should feel about the particular event/activity/topic.
3. Learner/trainee becomes capable of making value judgements on his own according to codes of conduct and principles now firmly established in his mind.

At the lowest level, the role of the learner/trainee is passive and limited to taking in information rather like a sponge with little personal concern. At the highest level, he will be integrating concepts, feelings and values into his own life/world.

You should help your learners/trainees to develop their feelings and values in such a way that they end up with desirable attitudes. In particular, consideration for all other road-users, especially the more vulnerable groups such as children, old people, invalids, cyclists etc., needs to be fostered.

Psychomotor domain (practical or physical skills) – This area is concerned with the learning of muscular and motor skills, such as co-ordination of the foot and hand controls, steering etc. At the lowest level, behaviour will be clumsy and hesitant with frequent errors. After following a well-designed training programme, and with practice, complete mastery should be achieved. The pupil should be able to drive to a reasonable standard without assistance from the instructor. The skilled performance will be efficient and flow smoothly, with only minor errors being made.

Many of the in-car driving skills will be dependent on SENSORIMOTOR skills. This is where the brain receives information from the senses (particularly through the eyes) and sends messages to the hands or feet to do whatever is necessary. KINAESTHESIS, which is the perception or consciousness of muscular movement, is particularly important when deciding on how much pressure to use on the accelerator or footbrake to suit the varying road and traffic conditions. Sensorimotor skills include touch, pressure (kinaesthetic sensitivity) and hand and body movements. For example:

The driver sees a pedestrian stepping off the pavement
⇓
Information is transmitted to the brain
⇓
The brain initiates a mirror check, followed by a stiffening of the arms and a foot movement to the brake
⇓
The foot presses the brake with a suitable amount of pressure.

The driving instructor who is teaching knowledge, understanding, skills and attitudes, will be utilising Bloom's three domains of learning every working day!

When taking a structured training course with a professional instructor, learning should be the result of a deliberate and directed effort. The learning plan should include:

- Learning to memorise things;
- Learning to understand things;
- Learning how to do things;
- Attitude development;

- Developing study skills.

These elements are covered in the following sections.

LEARNING TO MEMORISE THINGS

This is sometimes called ROTE LEARNING or PARROT-FASHION LEARNING and is the method by which most of us learnt our tables at school. Rote learning is rather limited in that it does not necessarily prove an understanding of the subject.

For example, a learner could memorise the overall stopping distances of a vehicle and be able to tell you 'The stopping distance if you are travelling at 30 miles per hour on a dry road would be 23 metres'. The learner should then be asked to point out something that is 23 metres away!

Even when the pupil can do this reasonably accurately, it is still necessary to test his ability to keep a safe distance from the car in front when driving at 30 miles per hour.

Knowledge in itself does not guarantee an UNDERSTANDING, nor the ability to use the knowledge and link it in with the skill of leaving sufficient distance between vehicles. Knowledge is often, therefore, just the starting point. The good instructor will need to use a skilful question and answer technique to verify understanding and test the pupil's ability to put the knowledge into practice.

This is sometimes known as VALIDATION: it involves proving that something has been understood by demonstrating the ability to carry it out.

Memory is vital for those learning to drive as it is no good learning something if two weeks, two years or twenty years later it has been forgotten.

The ability of your pupils to retain information and knowledge, and their capacity for forgetting what they have already learnt, will vary enormously from person to person. This is where the patience of a professional instructor will pay dividends as, with some pupils, there will be a need to explain things over and over again.

Up to the prime of life, the learning rate and the ability to retain information, knowledge and skills increase as the maturity level increases. After maturity both the learning rate and the ability to retain knowledge start to diminish.

Most learning requires the pupil to memorise things. Learning to drive is no exception. Your pupils will need to learn the sequences involved in approaching junctions, facts from the *Highway Code* and the criteria for carrying out the manoeuvring exercises.

Memorising something is the process of acquiring information, retaining it in the brain, and then being able to recall it at a later time. There are three components to your memory:

1. The sensory information storage system;
2. The short-term memory store;
3. The long-term memory store.

The sensory information storage system: This stage of the memory process involves the pupil in receiving information through the senses from the environment. In learning to drive this would be primarily through sight, hearing and touch. For example, watching a demonstration, listening to a briefing and feeling when the clutch is at biting point.

Sensory information is transmitted to the brain via the nervous system and much of it is only retained for a matter of minutes before being forgotten.

The short-term memory store: Some of the sensory information received by the brain is transferred to the short-term memory store, particularly sensory information which is familiar to the learner. Because the learner attaches importance to this information, it can be recalled immediately. Combined with other knowledge and perceptions already stored in the memory, the learner begins to understand what the senses are experiencing. The capacity of short-term memory is, however, relatively small.

The long-term memory store: The long-term memory has a much greater capacity and allows the learner to recall information that has been accumulated over a long period of time. Thus, it is the most important part of the memory, and also the most complex.

Long-term memory is vital in being able to drive safely in that it allows the driver to recall facts, solve problems and make decisions, sometimes all in a split second.

The more quickly the learner driver transfers information into his long-term memory, building on previous knowledge and understanding, the quicker he will learn to drive.

How can we help our learners to develop their long-term memories?
The first stage is to put the information in a form which can be more easily remembered by:

- breaking it down into its key components;
- using mnemonics – for example, MSM, PSL, LAD;
- painting pictures – 'What would happen if . . . ?';
- using word associations like 'ease the clutch', 'squeeze the gas' and 'creep and peep'; and
- using visual keys – for example, 'round signs give orders, triangular signs give warnings', 'think of the thickness of a coin'.

When you have translated the information into a more memorable form, you could write it down and ask your pupils to memorise it by rote. You could then check whether they have remembered it by asking questions at the beginning of the next lesson. If they have not learnt it, do not lose heart. Explain to them that it is difficult to learn and encourage them to do some more studying.

Repetition is a very good way of fixing information in the brain, but care should be taken to ensure that your repetition does not sound like 'nagging'.

You should encourage your pupils to study the *Highway Code*, *Your Driving Test* and *The Driving Manual*. You will then need to confirm that this has been done by testing their knowledge. You could set simple multiple-choice questions which could be given as homework, thus helping them to maintain interest in between their driving lessons.

There are some very good videos available which you could loan to your pupils for home use. This should also help to maintain their interest. If you do this, however, you must ensure that you are not infringing any copyright restrictions.

LEARNING TO UNDERSTAND SOMETHING

An effective way of finding out whether your pupils understand something, is to ask them to explain it to you: '*why* do we have to look round over our shoulder before moving off'; '*what* must we do when we get to our turning point *before* we begin to reverse round the corner, and *why*?'.

Understanding something means knowing its meaning, whether it be a statement of fact, a concept, or a principle. When a pupil is learning to do something, it is important that, to begin with, the key steps are understood, and then practice takes place until mastery has been achieved. ROTE LEARNING will be of little help to the pupil here and you need to use GESTALT LEARNING techniques (learning by understanding).

GESTALT LEARNING involves using mental processes as well as physical ones. It relies on the principle that the whole is greater than the sum of the parts. The easiest way to explain GESTALT LEARNING is to use the analogy of a piece of music. Many of us often remember a catchy tune, to such an extent sometimes that we cannot get it out of our head. It would be much more difficult, however, to remember just one phrase of that tune, even more difficult to remember just a few notes, and almost impossible to remember just one note, as this would depend on us having perfect pitch.

Beethoven is said to have conceived whole pieces of music in his head before setting about writing down the individual notes which, when all put together and played by an orchestra, became the beautiful pieces of music that were originally conceived.

To use an analogy in driving – if you were teaching a pupil how to approach a junction, or to turn right or left, you would outline the complete manoeuvre and then break it down into its component parts.

The learner would need to understand the Mirror–Signal–Manoeuvre routine, and then be able to break down the Manoeuvre part into the Position–Speed–Look–Assess–Decide routine. Not only would he need to understand all the *when*, *why*, *how* and *where*s pertaining to these sequences, he would also need to practice carrying them out until a reasonable degree of safety was achieved.

The GESTALT theory relies on the assumption that no matter how well the pupil understood and could carry out any component parts of the MSM PSL LAD routines, unless he could emerge from the junction safely, very little would have been achieved.

You would then need to go back to whichever of the component parts needed improving to make the whole routine effective. You may need to give more explanation, possibly a demonstration, and certainly more practice to improve the learner's performance.

All of the foregoing are dependent on the pupil's UNDERSTANDING.

> *There is little point in getting to the PRACTICE stage if the pupil does not UNDERSTAND what is expected of him.*

The starting point in teaching understanding is to:

1. Ask questions;
2. Solve problems.

1. Asking questions

When giving information to learners, you should ask yourself '*Why, when, where, how* does he need to do that?' You will then need to ask the pupil the same questions, or give them the reasons. The good instructor will probably use a mixture of asking and telling in order to make the lesson more varied. When using a question and answer routine, try not to make it sound like an INTERROGATION as this will only annoy or demoralise, and you may lose the pupil!

Try to relate any new information to what the pupil already knows (teaching from the known to the unknown). This will allow the pupil to build up a store of understanding. It is of little use for a pupil to know *how* and *when* to do something if he doesn't understand why it is important.

We have all had pupils come to us from other instructors, or those who have been taught by friends or relatives, who are making mistakes and do not understand why what they are doing is wrong. For example, you may get pupils who signal every time they move off when there are no other road users in sight. When you ask 'Why did you signal?' the reply is very often 'My dad says you must always signal before you move off.'

It is obvious from this response that there is no understanding of what signals should be used for, nor how and when to use them.

> *Your job is to explain why it is important to assess each situation on its own merits, and then decide whether a signal is required or not. You could confirm this by asking 'Who were you signalling to?'*

2. Solving problems

Problem solving is covered in more detail in section 6.2, but you need to know how solving problems will help your pupils to UNDERSTAND things.

Solving problems usually relies on the learner being able to transfer to new situations any knowledge and understanding already stored in the long-term memory. This should assist the learner in working out different possible solutions to a particular problem.

The learner can then evaluate these solutions and work out which is the most appropriate for the problem being dealt with.

> *To solve problems successfully, you will need to use intellectual skills to pose the appropriate questions which will enable the correct solution to be arrived at. Once the problem has been solved, it is easier to understand why it occurred in the first place and how to prevent it in the future.*

The technique of problem solving is particularly useful when analysing the driving errors made by learners, whether they be in the car (errors of control) or outside (errors of road procedure).

An example of this would be a learner driver turning left and swinging wide after the corner. The cause of the error might be obvious to the instructor, but not so obvious to the learner who may perceive several possible reasons for the error. Perhaps he began turning the steering wheel too late, misjudged the amount of lock needed for that particular corner, or approached the corner too fast, which meant that he didn't have time to steer accurately enough to maintain the correct position.

> *Having recognised the fault, the good instructor would help the pupil to analyse the fault by using the question and answer technique to arrive at the cause of it.*

The first question could be 'Why do you think you swung wide after the corner?' After a process of elimination, the pupil should eventually arrive at the correct answer.

Having solved the problem it would be necessary to take the pupil round the block in order to have another attempt at turning the same corner. You might choose to give the pupil a 'talk-through', particularly with regard to when to start braking and how much to brake, in order to ensure that the corner is negotiated more accurately. When success is achieved, the pupil should then be allowed to deal with similar corners unassisted, thus validating his understanding and skill.

This all sounds fairly logical when you put it down on paper. However, it is amazing how many instructors would, first of all, fail to pin-point accurately the cause of the error (not just the effect), and then not be able to assist the pupil in working out a solution to the problem, or to put the solution into practice.

In problem solving, INSIGHT LEARNING is the name given to the process which involves the learner in surveying each component of the problem and calling on previous knowledge to arrange the links into a sequence or chain. After examining all aspects of the problem, in a flash of INSIGHT, the solution suddenly becomes apparent. This is sometimes called the 'ahaa' technique because the flash of insight is often accompanied by the exclamation 'Ahaa!'.

An example of this would be somebody trying to work out why his car will not start. He checks the battery, the distributor cap, the points and then, when checking the plugs, discovers that one of the leads has come adrift. 'Ahaa!' he exclaims and then puts the plug lead back on, gets in, starts the engine: of course, it starts first time.

LEARNING TO DO SOMETHING (SKILL TRAINING)

In learning to drive, it is the practical application of the knowledge, understanding and attitudes gained that is most important. Whatever the situation, when learning to do something there are three basic steps needed:

1. Determine the purpose – WHAT and WHY
2. Identify the procedures involved – HOW
3. Practice the task – DO

1. Determine the purpose – WHAT and WHY

Learners must have a clear understanding of the reason for needing to be able to do whatever it is that you are teaching them. When teaching people how to drive the reasons why things are done in a certain way are invariably to do with:

Safety
Convenience
Efficiency
Simplicity
Economy

A simple example which encompasses most of the above would be using the brakes to slow the car rather than the gears:

- it is generally safer (you have both hands on the wheel, and the brake lights come on to warn people behind);
- it is more efficient (the car is slowing on all four wheels rather than just two);
- it is much easier (you have less to do if you cut out unnecessary gear changes);
- It is cheaper (brake pads and linings are cheaper than clutches and gearboxes).

2. Identify the procedures – HOW

The easiest way for the learner to understand how to do something is for the instructor to break the skill down into simple, manageable steps.

If it is a more complicated task, then the instructor should consider whether or not a DEMONSTRATION would benefit the pupil (see section 4.7 – Explanation, Demonstration, Practice routine).

3. Practice the task – DO

What I hear, I forget; What I see, I remember; What I do, I understand.

> *The driving instructor must never forget that it is the doing that will give the pupil the greatest* UNDERSTANDING. *In each driving lesson the instructor must therefore give the pupil as much time as possible to* PRACTICE *the skills which have been learnt.*

The more time spent in practising the skill, the more improved the performance should be. Good habits must be encouraged during practice as it is much more difficult to correct them once they have become built in to the routines used by the learner.

Every instructor knows that it is much simpler to teach correct procedures to somebody with no driving experience than it is to correct the mistakes of somebody who has received poor instruction.

Although some car driving routines could be taught initially by ROTE (for example, the MSM, PSL and LAD routines), the application of them requires an understanding which would be more easily acquired by using GESTALT methods, which allow the pupil to make connections with previously established principles.

For example, once a pupil has carried out one of the manoeuvres using the criteria of CONTROL, OBSERVATION and ACCURACY, it will be relatively simple for him to follow the same pattern in similar but slightly more complicated manoeuvres (teaching from the known to the unknown).

As an instructor the difficulty will be in mixing both ROTE and GESTALT methods to suit the needs of each individual pupil, combined with the all important PRACTICE.

The skill of the teacher is to find a mix which works, or be prepared to change to a different mixture if necessary.

> *The key to good instruction is the flexibility of the instructor to be able to work out what is best for the pupil, and adapt to suit.*

ATTITUDE DEVELOPMENT

Positively developing a driver's attitude is no different from developing the other transferable skills. You must have the correct attitude towards driving in order to be able to transfer a similar attitude to your learners.

You will need to develop your learner's assessment and decision making skills so that they become compatible with your own. Remember, you must be able to persuade learners how to do what you want them to do, in the way that you want them to do it. For example, do your learners:

- show courtesy and consideration for other road-users at all times?;
- reduce the risk of accidents by planning well ahead?;
- follow the rules in the *Highway Code*, keeping within the law?;
- think defensively instead of aggressively?; and
- always consider the consequences of unsafe actions?

Engendering correct attitudes in pupils is difficult, especially when teaching adults. Previous knowledge and learning can get in the way and old attitudes are difficult to modify.

The learner comes into this world with no attitudes about anything. Attitudes are formed early on, mainly by association with friends, relatives or groups with strong views on particular subjects. In the driving task, a learner who spends a lot of time as a passenger alongside a father who, for example, is a very aggressive driver will see this as being the norm and is likely to adopt a similar attitude when becoming a driver himself (see section 2.6 – Barriers to Learning).

When this learner realises that his attitude may be different to yours he may try to put on a show, just for the benefit of you or the driving examiner.

Attitudes are formed from three constituents:

KNOWLEDGE
MOTIVATION
EMOTION

The attitudes of learners can be changed by modifying their views and the decisions they make in any given situation by skilful persuasion.

To assist in this modification of attitude, you could use accident statistics regarding new drivers, safe driving videos, the high cost of insurance for newly qualified drivers etc.

> *There is little doubt that attitudes have an enormous influence on the behaviour of the driver and the development of favourable attitudes is probably the most effective long-term method of reducing road accidents.*

By far the most useful aid to attitude development is the continual use of the DEFENSIVE DRIVING theme, pointing out the safety benefits to your pupils.

Defensive driving

You can contribute positively towards reducing the risk of accidents by teaching your pupils defensive driving techniques and attitudes. The adoption of a defensive attitude is probably more important than skill development. It is very clever to be able to get out of trouble when a potentially dangerous situation arises, but it is much more clever to avoid getting into trouble in the first place!

The theory of defensive driving relies on research and statistics which show that human behaviour is generally motivated most powerfully by a desire to preserve one's own safety. Defensive driving develops this concept by instilling in drivers an attitude designed to do just that, coupled with the advanced observation of potential accident situations. It may be defined as 'driving in such a way as to prevent accidents, in spite of adverse conditions and the incorrect action of others'.

An accident has been described as 'an unforeseen and unexpected event', but in many cases potential road accidents *can* be foreseen and in most cases, when they happen, are caused by driver error. Everyone then asks who was to blame. Of far more value to driver education is to consider 'Was it preventable?'.

A preventable accident is one where a driver – not necessarily at fault – could reasonably have taken some action to prevent it happening.

The Driving Instructor's Handbook goes into more detail on hazard awareness, reducing risk and the theory of defensive driving. Some of the factors involved in road accidents are:

- visibility;
- weather conditions;
- road conditions;
- time of day;
- the vehicle; and
- the driver.

In this section we will be concentrating on the driver and how we can instil into our learners a 'defensive attitude'.

Human actions which may contribute to accident situations are:

- committing a traffic offence;
- abuse of the vehicle;
- impatience;
- sheer discourtesy; and
- lack of attention.

The defensive driver will consider all these factors, making a continuous and conscious effort to recognise each hazard in advance, understand the defensive attitude needed, and maintain the skill required to take preventive action in sufficient time.

You should encourage your pupils to drive with full concentration to avoid potential accidents caused by other drivers or road-users.

> *A constant awareness is required so that, no matter what they do, other people cannot get the drivers you have trained involved in an accident.*

If the other driver wants priority, train your drivers to let him have it – better a mature decision than a lifetime of suffering as the result of an accident. Teach your drivers how to avoid confrontation and keep a cushion of safe space around their vehicles at all times.

Get them to ask continually 'What if . . .?' – in this way they will improve their anticipation skills and be able to take defensive action before a situation develops into an accident.

Teach them to consider using the horn to let others know they are there. It is not in the British character to make a lot of noise, but just a gentle dab on the horn could prevent an accident. It is far better for your pupils to sound the horn to alert another person than not to sound it and have to carry out an emergency stop, especially if there is somebody else close behind.

As well as thinking defensively, favourable attitudes should be developed towards:

- vehicle maintenance and safety;
- traffic law (eg, safe use of speed, traffic signs and road markings, parking restrictions, drink/drive laws, dangerous driving implications);
- the more vulnerable groups of road-users;
- route planning and timing of journeys;
- reduced-risk driving strategies;
- further education and training for advanced/defensive driving; and
- learning and studying.

DEVELOPING STUDY SKILLS

You will need to develop your study skills because your self-development programme is dependent on studying. However, driving is mainly practical so you will be studying, literally, while 'on the job'.

You may at some stage in the future wish to gain extra qualifications or take some remedial or specialist training – this will also involve you in studying.

Your learners too will need to study between lessons. This will become even more essential when they have to take a separate Theory Test prior to the driving test. You will need to assist them in the studying and preparation process.

In developing study technique one needs to:

- make time available;
- find the right place; and
- formulate a study plan.

Making time available

You will have to emphasise the importance of revising between lessons and explain to pupils why they may need to reorganise any social activities so that their studying is effective.

The key is to help them establish a balance between each demand on the time they have available. They should not be forced to devote all of their time and energy to studying at the expense of other interests and activities as this may cause resentment.

You may also have to consider the needs of your pupils' families. One of the best ways of achieving this is to get the family involved with the studying, perhaps by helping to test the student's knowledge, or looking through any written work which has been done.

Time management is crucial. Whenever possible, exploit those times of the day when the student is in the best frame of mind for studying, scheduling any other interests around them.

Initially, the student should try out different times until a routine is established which allows time for studying alongside other demands.

The key ingredients contributing to the success of any studying are self-discipline and determination. Inability to sustain this motivation will make learning much less effective.

To reinforce this determination, the student should continually go through all the benefits which will be acquired after successfully completing the course of studying.

Finding the right place

This is almost as important as making the time available. The quality of learning is improved dramatically if the environment is 'conducive to learning'.

Certain types of learning – for example memorising information – require a quiet environment, free from distractions. For most people a room at home which is quiet and respected by other family members as a study room will be the best setting.

There needs to be space available for books etc, and a chair and table suitable for writing. Noise distractions should be kept to a minimum as they will reduce concentration and impede the learning process.

When a time and place for studying have been found, they should not be wasted. A structured approach to studying will give the best results.

Formulating a study plan
Studying is a skill which, like all skills, will improve with practice, determination and a planned approach.

Some people are naturally studious – they are content to spend hours at a time studying and reading. For others, studying requires effort. Other interests have to be shelved, distractions removed, and full concentration given to the task. To help in improving the quality of studying, the student needs a plan. For example the student should:

- set a personal objective and a time by which to achieve it;
- decide how much time each day/week will be needed to achieve the objective by the deadline set – the student should be guided by other learners/instructors/tutors as to how much time might be needed;
- prepare a formal study timetable for the duration of the learning programme, on which target dates for completing the component parts of the subject can be indicated;
- make sure the timetable includes relaxation time between study periods, with at least one whole free day per week and one or two study-free weeks if the programme is protracted;
- keep a continuous check on the progress made so as to adhere to the study timetable and not fall behind;
- not get dispirited if his studying falls behind but decide whether any leisure activity can be sacrificed to catch up with the study programme;

- not panic if pressures from studying build up, and discuss the pressure with friends, relatives, other students or instructors/tutors;
- consider lowering his sights and, perhaps, revise the timetable to extend the deadline if this is possible; and
- never let the study programme get on top of him, but keep on top of it!

2.6

BARRIERS TO LEARNING

There are many barriers to learning which the instructor has to overcome. As a general rule, the older the student, the greater the barriers. Don't forget that learning is the bringing about of more or less permanent changes in knowledge, understanding, skills and attitudes.

Adults will generally find that learning new skills and developing fresh attitudes is more difficult than acquiring knowledge and gaining understanding. In all of these areas, barriers to learning may have to be overcome.

The most common barrier encountered is that of previous learning.

Previous learning

Take the person who has developed a partial sense of speed as a passenger, perhaps being driven by an aggressive young company car driver. He will have subconsciously formed an impression of speed norms gained while sitting next to his friend. This could be detrimental when the novice tries to emulate the experienced driver. Unless dealt with in a sensitive but firm and positive way by the instructor, this could not only seriously hinder the progress of the learner but may also be dangerous.

Take the learner who comes to you from another instructor who is less up to date than you are, or who has received some 'lessons' from an elderly relative who has been driving for 50 years. He may have been misinformed. For example, two widely held – but false – conceptions are that it is good driving practice to:

- always change down progressively through the gears when slowing down or stopping; and
- always signal when moving off, passing parked cars and parking whether it is necessary or not.

Where the novice has been influenced by old-fashioned views it is likely to become a barrier to learning and cause conflict with the new information given by you.

When this type of interference occurs, you must find ways of convincing the pupil that a change in ideas is necessary, and considerable sensitivity, tolerance and patience will be needed during this period of 'unlearning'.

One of the ways of overcoming the problem would be to show the pupil the 'official view' in *The Driving Manual*. This will add weight to your words and help to convince the pupil that change is necessary.

Another way would be for you to prepare a balance sheet, listing the benefits of carrying out the correct procedure (your method) and then asking the pupil to write down all the benefits of carrying it out their way.

Lack of motivation is also a barrier to learning. However, where driving instruction is concerned, because of the costs involved, this is not a common problem (see section 2.2 – Motivation for Learning to Drive). You could have a pupil who is not paying for the lessons personally, such as somebody whose employer wishes him to pass the test in order to help with the firm's business activities, and this person may have no desire at all to learn to drive.

To overcome this lack of motivation, you would need to outline the personal benefits of learning and also the consequences of not keeping the boss happy!

Other barriers to learning are:

ILLITERACY,
DYSLEXIA,
COLOUR BLINDNESS,
LANGUAGE DIFFICULTY,
DEAFNESS, and
PHYSICAL DISABILITY.

Any problems with vision, speech, hearing, communication or physical disability should be noted on the driving test application form (DL26) so that an examiner who is qualified to deal with the problem can be made available.

ILLITERACY

Being unable to read and write can be a barrier to learning how to drive. However, the instructor who is prepared to adapt his teaching to suit the needs of the pupil can usually find ways of overcoming the problem.

Two-fifths of the world's population are deemed to be illiterate but, in northern Europe, the incidence of illiteracy is extremely rare. In the UK the most common situation is likely to be that of teaching people from the Gypsy community. These people often make up for their inability to read and write by being very practical and dextrous and frequently pick up driving with little or no instruction at all!

The instructor will need to use visual aids, discussion and demonstration to get the message across. It would also be useful to involve the pupil's family in assisting with study and learning. Help will be needed particularly with the *Highway Code*.

DYSLEXIA (WORD BLINDNESS)

The inability to read or not recognise certain words or letters is called dyslexia. Neither its cause nor its effects are easily explained. Partially genetic, it can be described as a disorganisation of the language area of the brain which, in turn, produces problems connecting sounds with visual symbols.

The net result is more readily understood. A dyslexic may experience learning difficulties with reading, writing and mathematics. Ignorance of dyslexia in the past branded its sufferers as stupid when they were anything but.

Dyslexia is uncommon and, again, should not present a problem to the instructor who is prepared to vary the instruction to suit the needs of the pupil. Visual aids should be used and help given in recognising and acting on traffic signs.

More help may be needed when learning *Highway Code* rules. The instructor should also try to encourage the pupil's family to help with the study.

Also, special computer games are now available to help people with dyslexia overcome some of the problems.

COLOUR BLINDNESS

This is only likely to cause a problem when dealing with traffic lights, pedestrian-controlled lights and road signs. Usually the learner will be able to distinguish when the lights are changing and their different positions, even though they may not be able to recognise the colours shown.

LANGUAGE DIFFICULTIES

If a pupil's understanding of English is very poor it can be a barrier to learning and, in extreme cases, the learner might need the help of an interpreter.

Providing the pupil has some knowledge of English, the use of visual aids, demonstrations and getting to know what the limitations are will help the instructor to overcome these difficulties.

It is important, right from the start, for the instructor to encourage pupils to say if there is anything they have not understood.

If there is someone in the family who speaks better English than the pupil, it may be useful to have a debriefing with them present. This should enable the instructor to clarify specific requests to the pupil and also allow the pupil to relate any queries to the instructor.

TEACHING DEAF PEOPLE TO DRIVE

The purpose of this section is to give guidelines which will help you to teach deaf people how to drive by adapting the PTS outlined in this book to suit their particular needs.

In this country there are some 50,000 people who have either been born deaf or who became deaf in early childhood. There are several thousand others who have become profoundly deaf in adult life after they have learnt to speak and write.

On entering school, most children will have a vocabulary of some 2,000 words. Children who cannot hear start school with hardly any vocabulary at all. They are unable to hear general conversation, they cannot obtain any information from the radio and they get only limited help from television. This all adds to the problems of communication which last a lifetime.

By the time a deaf youngster has reached the age of 17 and is thinking about learning to drive, he will have had most of his education in special schools or units; he will have some speech, but this may be difficult to follow except for close members of his family; and he will usually use sign language but, in addition, will be able to lip-read to a certain extent.

The deaf teenager may have a reading age well below his physical age and, consequently, his ability to read and write may be limited. He will often, however, be just as bright and intelligent as his peers with hearing and, with understanding and patience from you, will be able to assimilate all that is necessary to learn to drive.

> *Although not being able to hear will undoubtedly be a barrier to learning, an understanding of the deaf pupil's special problems will quickly enable you to overcome them.*

People who cannot hear do not regard themselves as being disabled. Indeed, deafness is not classed as a driver disability so no restrictions are placed on the full licence.

It is particularly important for deaf people, and those with no useful hearing at all, to disclose this fact in the 'Disabilities and special circumstances' box in the DSA application form for the driving test (DL26). This will ensure that the examiner will be prepared to modify the method of delivery of instructions to suit the candidate's particular needs.

If the learner has neither hearing nor speech, he will be allowed an interpreter – the interpreter will sit in the front seat while the examiner sits in the back during the *Highway Code* questions.

When no interpreter is to be present, you must find time to talk to the examiner well before the date of the test so that you can explain which method has been used to give directions and instructions during training. The examiner can then make his own directions and instructions compatible, which will mean that the pupil on test is much more likely to be relaxed.

Unfortunately, you will not often be asked to teach deaf people how to drive and, if asked, you may be reluctant to do so. This is mainly because there is a widespread lack of understanding of the problems of deaf people and the way in which they are able to communicate effectively with others: for your part, the task may seem too daunting. As a result, people without hearing often find it difficult to obtain expert tuition and tend to rely on amateurs such as parents and friends – people who may be good at communicating with deaf people but are not necessarily qualified to teach safe driving for life. Driving instructors who are specialists in the art of communication, have good PTS, and who understand the effects of not being able to hear, are better equipped to teach deaf people than friends and relatives.

After adapting your PTS to teach deaf people how to drive, you will find the experience both rewarding and enriching. The problem for you will be to learn the best way to transfer your knowledge, skill, understanding and attitude, to the pupil.

PTS for teaching deaf people how to drive
It is not necessary for you to learn the British sign language used by deaf people, but you must use simple straightforward words which have only one meaning, avoiding those which may be ambiguous. For example, if the deaf pupil lip-reads the word 'right' when you mean 'OK' he might think that you are asking him to turn right or move to the right.

As lip-reading depends as much on the clarity of the speaker's lip movements as on the ability of the deaf person, it is essential that you speak slowly and distinctly, and move your lips to form each word. Face-to-face conversation while stationary becomes more important than with a hearing pupil. Never shout – the pupil cannot hear what you are saying!

With impaired hearing, sight and touch become a great deal sharper and this will help the deaf pupil to overcome the disadvantage of not being able to hear. The deaf learner is likely to be much more aware of what is happening on the road ahead and will quickly master how to assess risk.

People without hearing also develop great sensitivity of feeling over the normal course of living in silence. Consequently, they often acquire clutch control and co-ordination with the accelerator fairly easily.

The powers of concentration of deaf pupils are often far better than those of many hearing pupils. Pupils who cannot hear do not lack intelligence: they are eager to learn and, once they have been taught something, are less likely to forget it.

An unsatisfactory response is more likely to be your fault than that of the pupil. Therefore, extra patience will be required from both of you.

> *Because of their lack of hearing it is vital that any communication, whether by visual aids or sign language, be reinforced by demonstrations.*

The normal skill training steps of EXPLANATION, DEMONSTRATION and PRACTICE must be followed but, because of the risk of danger arising from misunderstanding, the EXPLANATION needs to be more thorough than it would be when teaching a hearing pupil. The learner without hearing must fully understand all the safety implications of any driving skill before being allowed to practice the task.

At the beginning of the first driving lesson, it is vital that you both establish and agree what means of communication will be used.

Pre-prepared cards which cover *what, how, when* and, most importantly, *why* can be used. The cards can be used to reinforce the KEY POINTS of any manoeuvre or exercise with drawings of pedestrians cyclists and cars indicating the involvement of other road users. A magnetic board can be useful to recreate situations quickly and easily.

When giving directions, a simple form of sign language can be used provided you both agree and understand the signs to be used. These signs, because they are being used while the vehicle is moving along the road, will not be the same as those used in the British sign language. This must be explained to, and fully understood by, the pupil. For example, putting a thumb up will mean 'good', whereas putting a thumb down will mean 'bad'.

As a large amount of learning will take place through the eyes, it must be understood how the task of teaching deaf people becomes easier with the use of visual aids and demonstrations. Visual aids are not only invaluable, they are essential. (See section 4.6 – The Use of In-car Visual Learning Aids).

Face-to-face conversation, simple language and written notes should cover all of the other needs of the deaf pupil.

Diagrams such as those in the *Autodriva visual teaching system*, published by Margaret Stacey and available from Autodriva, will be invaluable when teaching deaf pupils how to drive. A complete practical teaching booklet has been produced by Elwyn Reed MBE which explains in detail a system for teaching deaf people how to drive. This is recommended to all those who are considering extending their PTS by undertaking this worthwhile activity. Details of the booklet, which has been approved by The British Deaf Association, are available from:

> The Institute of Master Tutors of Driving
> 12 Queensway
> Poynton
> Cheshire   SK12 1JG
>
> *Telephone*: 01625 872708

The diagrams and illustrations in this booklet together with your own visual aids and PTS will be of great assistance when teaching deaf people.

It is important to acquaint pupils with all the safety requirements of the L test outlined in the DSA publication *Your Driving Test*. Ensure that they completely understand what is expected from them when carrying out the set manoeuvres, particularly regarding the observations to be made.

Learning the *Highway Code*

The DSA video on the *Highway Code* will be useful so that pupils can study it in between lessons. Questions can be devised in written form to test their understanding of the rules.

Always have a writing pad handy so that any questions and answers can be written down.

If any problems arise, you will benefit from talking to the parents or relatives of pupils and getting in touch with any local associations for deaf people or:

> The British Deaf Association
> 38 Victoria Place
> Carlisle, Cumbria
> CA1 1HU
>
> *Telephone*: 01228 48844

PHYSICAL DISABILITY

Physical disability need not be a bar to driving. There are thousands of people with disabilities, some quite severe, who have passed the Driving Test. Many have proved their skill by also passing an advanced test.

Teaching people with disabilities to drive can be very rewarding as they usually have lots of motivation to learn and often put in more effort than their able-bodied peers.

If you do accept the challenge, the PTS in this book will help you to improve the quality of learning taking place. In particular, you will need to pay special attention to the following:

- *Flexibility* – being able to adapt your usual teaching methods to suit the perceived needs of the pupil.
- *Lesson planning* – being prepared to build in rest breaks and taking care not to spend too long on manoeuvres which may put physical strain on the pupil.
- *Body language* – watching carefully for signs of strain.
- *Feedback* – offering feedback only on things that are controllable. Telling the pupil that the reason he is not reversing in a straight line is because he is not turning around enough in the seat is not very helpful if he is unable to turn any more because of his disability.

Unless you have a large catchment area, fitting out a vehicle with lots of modifications to suit a wide variety of disabilities can be prohibitively expensive. Sometimes an automatic vehicle may be all that is needed to overcome the problems of some disabilities.

Three fairly common disabilities which can be overcome relatively simply, enabling the driving instructor to teach effectively, are:

- having only one leg;
- having only one arm; and
- restriction of head, neck or body movement.

Someone with no left leg should be able to drive an ordinary automatic vehicle, while somebody with no right leg will be able to get pedal extensions/adaptations to enable the accelerator and brake of an ordinary automatic vehicle to be operated with the good leg.

Someone with only one arm should also be able to drive an automatic vehicle with a steering spinner fitted. These can be fitted or removed in a matter of minutes with a screwdriver.

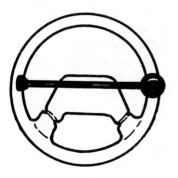

Steering wheel spinner

There are a number of different types of spinner to suit the individual needs of the person. See examples below:

Different types of steering spinners

Using this type of adaptation means that your own automatic driving school vehicle could be used to teach the disabled person and the steering spinner easily removed for use with able-bodied pupils.

For those with restricted movement of the head, neck or body, special mirrors may be fitted to remove the need to look round before moving off or changing lanes.

Those people wishing to learn to drive who have quite severe disabilities will normally seek an assessment from specialists at one of the mobility centres around the country. A list of these is included in *The Driving Instructor's Handbook*. If it is considered that they will be able to learn successfully, they will be advised on how a suitable vehicle of their own could be adapted to help overcome their problems. Lessons will, in these cases, be conducted in the pupil's vehicle.

You may need to allow extra time at the beginning and end of lessons for the pupil to get in and out of the vehicle. Frequent breaks may be necessary during lessons if the pupil is prone to tiring easily or becomes uncomfortable after sitting in the same position for a while.

> *You will need to assess each pupil's personal requirements, and adapt your teaching methods to suit them.*

Some people tire very easily as the day progresses. Lessons should be arranged at appropriate times so that they will be 'at their best' and as much learning as possible can take place. You will need to find out pupils' weaknesses and strengths and work out the best ways of dealing with them so that problems are minimised.

If you wish to specialise in this kind of work, it is recommended that you attend a course for instructors in teaching the disabled. These are conducted at the Banstead Mobility Centre in Carshalton, Surrey (Tel: 0181-770 1151).

IMPAIRMENT

Mere discomfort can be a barrier to learning. You need to be able to recognise whether or not your pupils are comfortable. Discomfort can have many causes, ranging from toothache to sitting in an incorrect position, or being told 'You must keep your heel on the floor when using the clutch' when either your foot is too small or your legs too long for you to do this comfortably.

Allowances may have to be made for very tall people – they will need the seat as far back as possible with the back rake adjusted to give more leg room. If you have a very small car it may even be necessary for you to advise them to take lessons with another instructor who has a larger car with more headroom.

Pupils of small stature may be assisted by securing cushions underneath and behind them, and pedal extensions may be needed for those with short legs or small feet. Your terminology may also need to be adjusted to allow for pupils not being able to keep their heel down when controlling the clutch.

If a pupil is not driving as well as usual there may be some simple explanation. For example, did he adjust the driving seat when he got into the car or was he in too much of a hurry to 'get going'. Make sure these minor procedures are carried out correctly otherwise you may both be at a loss as to the cause of the problems and the lesson may be wasted.

If the pupil is having an uncharacteristically bad lesson, it may be due to something as simple as wearing different shoes, or as complicated as having problems at home.

Ask tactfully if you think a pupil may not be feeling well. The lesson may be completely wasted if a minor illness is causing a distraction. You could even be aiding and abetting an offence if the pupil is taking drugs which affect driving.

Other barriers to learning to drive can be caused by the use of alcohol which, as well as being illegal, can cause a false sense of confidence and impetuous risk-taking. If you think a pupil has been drinking, ask tactfully and abort the lesson if necessary. On no account do you let the pupil take the test if they have been drinking.

Anxiety, emotion and stress can all affect concentration. If a pupil's driving is not up to the usual standard and they have recently had personal problems, it may be advisable to postpone the lesson. Explain that it is not the best time to drive as they will not be able to concentrate on the road and traffic environment.

We are all affected by the ageing process. For those who decide to learn to drive later on in life the going can be difficult. You should explain that it will be harder to learn and remember new procedures. Things may be more easily forgotten and concentration more difficult to sustain. Problems may be even greater for those in this age group who have decided to learn to drive because they have lost a partner or close relative. You will need lots of patience and understanding if you are to help these pupils attain their goal.

Continually assess your own effectiveness by asking yourself:

- Do I stress the benefits of learning to drive in order to motivate my pupils?
- Do I structure my teaching to make it easier for them to memorise things; understand things; and do things?

- Do I pay enough attention to developing or modifying their attitude towards driving and other road users?
- Do I help them to develop their studying skills, setting them enough 'between-lesson tasks'?
- Do I help them to overcome any barriers to learning which they may have?

3

Verbal and Non-Verbal Communication Skills

People learn all the time. If you did not learn you could not deal with the environment in which you live and work. You would constantly stub your toe on the foot of the bed, burn your fingers when cooking and press the wrong button when adjusting the television set.

Because the driving task is both difficult and potentially dangerous, driving instructors should accelerate the learning process for their pupils. You should ensure that you teach your pupils to understand the hazards and deal with them as soon as possible. In this chapter we will be concentrating on the essential Practical Teaching Skills (PTS) of communication used when teaching people how to drive which will help to bring about learning. These PTS include verbal, non-verbal and listening skills.

The Driving Standards Agency (DSA) considers that Approved Driving Instructors should be:

- ARTICULATE;
- ENTHUSIASTIC;
- ENCOURAGING;
- FRIENDLY;
- PATIENT; and
- CONFIDENT.

During the ADI Part 3 test of instructional ability and the periodic Check Test, these characteristics must be demonstrated and are assessed. Most of these INSTRUCTOR CHARACTERISTICS will be displayed while the instructor is communicating with pupils during driving lessons.

3.1

SPEECH

In this section we will consider the elements of speech which you can employ and how you can use your voice to communicate more effectively. While using speech to communicate ideas and information, you may also convey your innermost feelings and emotions, either deliberately or inadvertently.

The driving instructor must ensure that he uses speech effectively and in such a way that the pupil will hear what the instructor needs him to hear. For example, even though you may be frustrated or exasperated, you may not want your tone of voice to convey this to your pupil. There are, however, certain times when for safety reasons, you have to get your point across very forcefully. The elements of speech which will help you to communicate effectively are:

- tone of voice;
- use of emphasis;
- content of speech;
- use of figurative language;
- use of humour;
- speed of speaking;
- use of pronunciation;
- pitch of your voice; and
- use of inferred speech.

We shall consider the importance of each of these elements and the way you can best use them to improve your verbal communication.

THE TONE OF YOUR VOICE

When you speak to your pupils it is important to put them at ease and maintain their interest and attention. If they are not paying attention, it is doubtful whether they will learn anything at all.

Your tone of voice conveys your emotions and feelings, such as annoyance and pleasure, and supports the content of what you are saying. As the tone of voice often conveys the true meaning of your message, it is important that you sound friendly and relaxed even though you may be feeling the opposite!

Consider the following question: 'Why did you slow down?'. If you pose this question in a harsh tone of voice, you will sound as though you are telling the pupil off. If you ask the same question with a soft tone of voice, you are showing interest in their actions.

> *Practice asking the question in different ways and attempt to convey different meanings to it.*

When teaching you need to consider the tone of your voice not only to give a clearer meaning to the words themselves, but also to add variety to the speech in order to keep the pupil interested and attentive. If you stick to one tone only your voice will become MONOTONOUS which will soon cause the pupil to lose interest.

THE USE OF EMPHASIS

By putting greater stress on certain words you can alter the meaning of a sentence. For example:

> '*What* are you looking for?'
> 'What *are* you looking for?'
> 'What are *you* looking for?'
> 'What are you *looking* for?'
> 'What are you looking *for*?'

Practice asking this question out loud and, each time, put the emphasis on the word in italics. In the first question, you are asking about the action of looking itself. In the second you imply disbelief that the pupil is bothering to look at all. The third sentence queries whether it is the pupil who should be looking – perhaps somebody else should be looking! In the fourth example you are questioning the action – perhaps there is no point in looking at this moment in time. In the last question you are probing the pupil's understanding of what needs to be seen as a result of looking.

Now try using each of the questions again, continuing to emphasise the word in italics, but try to vary your voice to express concern, anger, and amazement.

As well as saying the words in a particular way you can sometimes stress a particular consonant or vowel to accentuate your meaning. For example, 'Slooowwwlly let the clutch come up'.

People who are practised and skilled speakers, such as politicians or lawyers, often use emphasis to considerable effect not only to help the listener to understand the message but also to indicate hidden meanings which otherwise might not have been obvious. Sometimes it is only when a speech is heard rather than read that you understand what message is being conveyed.

THE CONTENT OF SPEECH

As well as the tone and emphasis you use when speaking, the words themselves are vital if you wish to be effective in communicating.

We will be covering explanations, instructions and directions later in this chapter because the use of an unambiguous vocabulary is vital when teaching people how to drive. You should always try to match the words you are using to the level of understanding and ability of the pupil. The skilled trainer will be able to put trainees at their ease by talking with them at their own level.

> *There is no point in using long and complicated words when teaching somebody who cannot understand them. The best advice is to keep it simple, as this is more likely to bring about learning.*

Getting to know your pupils will help you to use suitable words which they will understand. A common criticism of poor instructors is that they use words which are above the heads of their pupils.

The use of jargon and technical language should be avoided unless perhaps you are dealing with a car mechanic. Even then you could get in deep water as he may know more than you do!

When dealing with the controls of the car it is best to explain to the pupil not only what the control does and how it is used, but the words which you are going to use when dealing with that control. This will avoid your pupil becoming confused with possibly dangerous results. For example, if you are going to call the accelerator the gas pedal don't suddenly confuse the pupil by calling it the 'throttle'.

While communicating with pupils, you should avoid talking about race, religion, sex and politics. Remarks of this nature may be offensive to the person in question and, even if they are not, they will devalue whatever else you may be saying, causing the pupil to 'switch off'.

THE USE OF FIGURATIVE LANGUAGE

Always try to make the content of your message interesting to listen to. There is nothing worse than boring your pupil. You can avoid doing this in a number of ways by using FIGURATIVE LANGUAGE. By this, we mean using such things as:

- METAPHORS;
- SIMILES;
- HYPERBOLE;
- ANALOGIES; and
- PERSONAL EXPERIENCES.

A METAPHOR is used to infer a similarity between things or situations which are not really associated – for example, 'crawling along at a snail's pace'.

A SIMILE is a figurative comparison using terms such as 'like' or 'as'. An example would be to say that a bad driver was 'driving like a lunatic'.

HYPERBOLE is the use of deliberate over-exaggeration – for example, 'That gap is big enough to get a bus through'. (You must be careful when doing this that your pupil does not take you literally!)

An ANALOGY is a comparison made to show a similarity in situations or ideas – for example, 'If you have time to walk across, then you will have time to drive across!'.

PERSONAL EXPERIENCES (or ANECDOTES) allow you to compare situations happening now with those which might have happened before. For example, if you had a pupil who tried to emerge unsafely, you might say, 'I had a pupil last week who tried to emerge from a junction without looking. If I hadn't used the dual controls, we would have hit a cyclist!'

By using all of these figures of speech you will make your lesson more interesting and the message is less likely to be forgotten, but care must be taken that you do not overuse them to the extent that the intended content of your message is diluted or lost.

You could also use research findings or refer to some respected authority such as the Department of Transport or the Driving Standards Agency to help you to add weight to your words.

THE USE OF HUMOUR IN SPEECH

Instructors who are humorous often maintain their pupil's attention and interest very effectively but it does not work for every pupil or every instructor. If you try to be funny unsuccessfully you could lose your credibility. We all know someone who when telling a joke invariably forgets the punchline. You should not tell jokes during the lesson time as this will annoy most pupils, and in no circumstances should you tell racist, sexist, religious or dirty jokes.

Many instructors can be extremely amusing without telling jokes. They can put a message across using wittiness but, again, not every pupil will respond well to witty remarks and some may take offence, especially if they do not realise that you are trying to be witty. You can often bring a smile to your pupil's face without trying too hard just by being alert and responding to a possibly difficult situation with a humorous remark. For example, you might be waiting at traffic lights which turn to green and your pupil does not move – you could gently ask 'What colour are we waiting for?'.

Unless the pupil is sarcastic himself, you should avoid using sarcasm. It could cost you a pupil!

THE SPEED OF SPEAKING

The speed at which you speak can help to maintain the interest of your pupils. You can create anticipation by increasing the speed of speech as you build up to an important point. You can also use silence, or pauses to allow things to sink in before you continue. If you pause while you are talking you can indicate a sense of deliberateness to give emphasis to certain key points. For example: 'MIRROR (pause), SIGNAL (pause), MANOEUVRE'.

You can also use pauses to give you time to think before delivering your next piece of information, but such pauses should not be excessive otherwise you will lose your pupil's attention completely. Try not to fill in the pauses with 'ums' and 'ahs' as this will irritate your pupil and detract from what you are saying.

Slowing down the speed at which you say a single word can be useful in indicating the speed of action required by matching it with the speed of the delivery of the word. For example, 'Slooowwwllyy let the clutch up, squeeeezze the gas' or 'Geennntttly brake'.

THE USE OF PRONUNCIATION

It is important that as an 'expert' you pronounce the words you use correctly. Your pupil will expect you to be fully conversant with the subject you are talking about and if you mispronunciate too often you could damage your credibility, distract your listeners from what you are saying and reduce their attention. If you come across new words when reading books on driving and intend using them but are unsure of their pronunciation, then it is best to refer to a dictionary.

For example, when teaching the emergency stop many instructors mispronounce the word 'cadence' as in cadence braking. Try looking it up in your dictionary and see if you are pronouncing it correctly!

THE PITCH OF YOUR VOICE

Pitch is a combination of the tone that you use and the loudness of the sound that you make. Considerable emphasis can be given to the instruction or direction you are giving by varying the pitch of your voice. Pitch is particularly useful when you wish to convey urgency, caution or importance either to whatever it is that you are saying or the way you wish your pupil to react to the words you are using.

Care must be taken not to over-exaggerate the pitch of your voice because it can be a distraction to your pupil. Your speech should be a comfortable variation of harsh and soft tones and of loudness and softness.

Speaking loudly will not always get the attention you desire. You only have to think of British tourists abroad trying to communicate with somebody with no English. In vain they end up almost shouting – *'DO YOU SPEAK ENGLISH?'*!

Pitch is useful when using key word prompts, particularly those which require urgent action such as 'WAIT', 'HOLD BACK' or 'STOP'.

THE USE OF INFERRED SPEECH

Inferred speech can be used to convey your feelings and especially your attitude to a given situation. The dictionary meaning of the words you are using is not as important as what they imply. For example, as a driving school proprietor you might say to one of your instructors: 'I see you're working 50 hours again this week Bill!'. The fact that you are saying this indicates to Bill that you are aware that his work pattern has changed. The way in which you deliver the message will indicate to Bill either your approval or disapproval.

> *It is therefore not only the words being used but also the way in which they are delivered that gets the message across.*

Inferred speech will sometimes be used to 'break the ice'. For example, if you ask 'How are you today Jason?', it not only puts Jason at ease but also gives you some feedback which might be useful when structuring the lesson content and the way in which you will 'handle' Jason. If he is feeling good, then perhaps you will set the objective for the lesson high. If Jason is not feeling good then perhaps your sights will be lowered to maybe consolidating an existing skill.

When meeting people for the first time, one often talks about the weather or the journey they have had to get to the meeting. The person opening the conversation might not genuinely be interested in these things but is really saying 'I wish to communicate with you, please respond.'

All of the above elements of speech can be developed. Whether teaching in the car, in the classroom or speaking to larger groups at meetings, conferences etc, it may be useful either to tape record or, better still (because you can also see what visual impact you are having), video the proceedings with a view to assessing and improving your performance.

There are certain speech distractions which should be eliminated where possible. The most common is the frequent use of speech mannerisms such as 'OK', 'right', 'you know', 'I mean', 'well then'. This trait gives the impression of a lack of confidence or nervousness, neither of which will help to put the pupil at ease or inspire trust. Also, the use of the word right to mean correct could be misleading and dangerous.

Talking plays a great part in teaching people how to drive and you should take every opportunity to further develop your speaking skills. Remember that, when speaking, you are not only giving a verbal message but also conveying your feelings and attitudes.

> *By varying your speech you can drastically change your listener's interpretation of what you are saying, whether you are talking on a one-to-one basis, or to small or large groups.*

Other common mistakes that speakers make which, particularly when they are talking to groups, can cause their listeners to become bored and lose their concentration are:

* repeating things which they have said before; and
* getting too technical for the audience.

Many older people begin to lose their short-term memory and repeat the same stories or anecdotes over and over again. Think about what you are saying and try to avoid using stories you have used before at other meetings. An audio or video tape recording of the speech will help you to do this.

Listening to a complex or statistical topic can be boring and the audience may switch off or even worse fall asleep. If you think you may be losing your audience then try a change of activity. For example, get the audience involved in a discussion, or use some good visual aids. Ask questions of the audience which will help to validate what you are saying.

Other specific types of verbal communication include social conversation, presenting a lesson, giving explanations, instructions and directions, most of which will be covered later in this chapter.

Telephone conversations form a valuable part of your life given that the initial contact with a potential customer is often made on the telephone. Much of what has been said about speech also applies.

The problem is that you are unable to read the body language of the person you are speaking to. If you cannot see the gestures and facial expressions of the other party you lose some insight into what they are thinking while they are speaking.

> *Communicating is not just talking, but should be a two-way exchange of ideas and information. You will therefore need to develop your listening skills.*

Listening skills are covered in section 3.7.

Developing the communication skills of speaking and listening will help you in presenting a driving lesson. Similar rules will apply to presentations to larger groups but in the next section, we are going to concentrate on the one-to-one lesson.

3.2

PRESENTING A LESSON

In this section we will discuss the PTS required when presenting a driving lesson. At some stage in your career you may also have to give presentations to a small or large group and the same PTS will again be helpful. However, a one-to-one presentation requires specialist skills.

Any presentation is much more likely to achieve its objectives if the presenter has done sufficient preparation:

POOR PREPARATION $\Rightarrow$ POOR PRESENTATION

Few driving instructors go into the lesson with a proper plan. The danger in this is, as Rudyard Kipling once said, 'If you don't know where you are going, no road will lead you there!'.

In section 7.4 we will be covering the specific requirements for presenting a lesson during the ADI Part 3 test. In that situation, the supervising examiner will actually set the objectives for the lesson and determine the character of the pupil. There is also a limitation on time (approximately 28 minutes).

With a real pupil on a real driving lesson, it is your responsibility to set the objectives and plan the use of time, taking into account the specific needs of the pupil. Unless dealing with a new one, the instructor usually has the advantage of knowing his pupil.

The easiest way to plan a lesson is first of all to think of the pupil and his level of ability. Then ask yourself the crucial 'teaching' questions – WHAT?, WHY?, HOW?, WHERE? and WHEN?

WHAT does the pupil already know? WHAT are we going to teach, and WHY do we need to teach it? HOW are we going to get the message across? WHERE do we need to go to carry out the main part of the lesson, and WHEN should we get to the main content of the lesson. (And, HOW are we going to manage the time available?)

Only when you have answered all of these questions can you get to work in planning the lesson and delivering the presentation.

Modern thinking in education is that any lesson should be structured with the pupil in mind. This is known as PUPIL CENTRED LEARNING. For you and your pupil to achieve your separate objectives, you will need to involve the pupil, and the following communication skills will help you to do this.

BRINGING THE LESSON TO LIFE

To help maintain the interest and attention of your pupil you need to bring the lesson to life, personalising it and making it enjoyable. At the end of the lesson, the pupil should get out of the car feeling not only that he has learnt something and achieved his objective but also that he has enjoyed himself.

Fifty per cent of your pupils will probably come to you from other instructors. Why is this? It is usually because the pupil felt that he was not getting anywhere with his previous instructor or he was not enjoying his lessons.

Don't forget that each pupil is an individual. Use first names during the lesson and make eye contact when discussing things while stationary. Use the different speech elements we discussed in the previous section – metaphors, hyperbole and similes – to add interest and perhaps a touch of humour to the presentation.

Use visual aids when explaining things, and make sure that the pupil can actually *see* what it is that you are showing them. So many instructors cover up what they are showing with their hands so the pupil cannot see or understand the points they are making!

Visual aids will be covered in more detail in section 4.6. They will help you to bring the presentation to life.

Another way to make the lesson more interesting for pupils is to INVOLVE them as much as possible by using the 'question and answer' technique.

PUPIL PARTICIPATION THROUGH QUESTION AND ANSWER ROUTINES

We have already talked about you asking yourself questions to help you plan the lesson. We now need to ask similar questions during the presentation to ensure that the pupil is participating.

Your purpose in using questions is to motivate the pupil by challenging or intriguing him, helping him to work out solutions and reasons for doing things by himself.

The best questions to use are OPEN-ENDED QUESTIONS which must be answered with some information rather than a 'Yes' or 'No'. For example, if you ask a pupil if he has understood your explanation of something, he can only reply 'Yes' or 'No'. This still does not tell you whether he has actually understood it. You would therefore need to ask further questions to decide whether he has understood it or not.

Open-ended questions usually begin with the words: WHY, WHEN, HOW, WHO, WHERE, WHAT and WHICH. They are all fairly easy to remember because they begin with the letter W – except, of course, for the word HOW.

The weakest word to use is WHICH because this could be answered with a guess. You would then need to ask another question to find out if the pupil had simply guessed correctly.

The most powerful teaching word is WHY. For example, if you asked your pupil which signs are the most important, round ones or triangular ones and the pupil answered 'Round ones' you would then need to ask the question 'Why are round signs more important than triangular ones?'. It would have been better to have asked that question in the first place.

You should always try to ask a question which will give you the answer that you are looking for. The idea is not to baffle pupils but to help them to work things out for themselves.

Open-ended questions can be used on the move to test a pupil's awareness of approaching hazards and what action should be taken. However, they should not require lengthy answers or a discussion. You can sometimes ask two questions at once – for example, 'What does this sign mean, and how are you going to deal with it?'.

Questions which require a long answer or a discussion should only be used when parked at the roadside somewhere safe and convenient.

Avoid asking questions while a pupil is trying to negotiate a junction or other hazard. This will only confuse him and could cause him to lose concentration and make a mess of things.

The skill of the instructor is to choose questions wisely to get the pupil thinking and involved in decision making.

You should always confirm your pupil's understanding of what has been explained by careful use of the question and answer technique. Think about how you phrase the question:

- use simple wording that can be easily understood; and
- make sure the questions are answerable and reasonable.

It is no good posing a question which could be answered with any number of replies. Do not use trick questions which will only undermine the confidence of the pupil, make them feel foolish and defeat the objective of the question.

Most driving instructors are very good at telling their pupils what to do and how to do it, but very few ensure that learning and understanding have taken place by skilful use of the question and answer technique. As well as using questions yourself, invite questions from your pupil – 'Is there anything you are not sure about?'.

Never ASSUME that your pupil has understood everything you have said!

At the end of each lesson, when analysing your own performance, ask yourself whether the questions you used during the lesson achieved their objective.

GIVING AND GAINING FEEDBACK

Feedback is an important part of the learning process.

Feedback at its simplest is where, for example, the driver hears an ambulance approaching from behind and pulls over to let it pass. Another example would be when the 'feel' from a flat tyre alerts the driver to the fact that something is wrong.

Giving and gaining feedback are useful PTS, especially when teaching on a one-to-one basis or in small groups.

Feedback is usually preceded by an enquiry, a prompt or a physical action. For example, the facial expression of a pupil after having carried out a manoeuvre will often give a good indication of how well they feel they have done.

Feedback is obtained and 'fed back' to the initial prompter as a direct result of the initial action. It can be given verbally, physically or sometimes by body language, and can relate both to people and machinery.

In the driving instruction experience, feedback can occur from:

- the car to the pupil/instructor, eg engine labouring;
- the pupil to the instructor;
- the instructor to the pupil;
- the pupil to other road users;
- other road users to the pupil;
- the examiner to the pupil;
- the pupil to the examiner;
- the trainer to the trainee;
- the trainee to the trainer.

Using a question-and-answer routine is only one way of giving and obtaining feedback.

When teaching learner drivers you should give feedback on what they are doing well and what may need improving. Just as important is finding out from the pupil how well *they* think they are doing. They might think they are doing brilliantly when they are really struggling. Alternatively, they might think they need extra lessons on a particular item whereas you might think they are unnecessary. Every pupil will benefit from extra lessons, so never discourage them from booking more if they feel they need them.

Many driving instructors do not understand feedback and give instead constant criticism, which only destroys what confidence pupils may have and leaves them feeling dejected and wanting to give up.

Many potentially good drivers give up because they do not receive support and encouragement from their instructors. Invariably these pupils will start learning again, as they really need to drive. However, they nearly always go to a different instructor. Never forget that if you are not fulfilling the needs of your pupils, there are plenty more instructors for them to choose from.

Feedback should therefore be offered in a sensitive way, so as not to hurt the feelings of the pupil.

A number of guidelines need to be followed when giving feedback to your pupils.

- Always give positive feedback. Rather than only telling them what needs improving, give praise for what they are doing well.
- Give encouragement before giving criticism.
- Give feedback in a helpful way rather than in a judgmental way (eg, rather than saying 'You will fail your test if you do that!', try 'If you let the clutch up more smoothly, your passengers will find the drive much more comfortable').
- Only offer feedback on those things that are controllable. Telling the pupil that he cannot turn the wheel properly because he is too fat will not solve the problem.
- Do not give critical feedback without offering a remedy for the problem.

Hopefully the guidelines above will help you to give feedback in a 'human' way, as this will build the confidence of the pupil and his confidence in your ability to teach him!

After each lesson, analyse any feedback you have given. Decide whether you could have improved the way in which you presented the feedback to your pupil.

Think carefully about how your pupil reacted to the feedback. Did you tell the pupil what they had done well or did you just criticise their driving?

3.3

GIVING BRIEFINGS AND EXPLANATIONS

Driving instructors will often need to give BRIEFINGS to their pupils which explain what is to be covered during the lesson to come. These briefings will usually include a statement of the objectives for the lesson, and a short summary of the key points of WHAT is to be covered.

The briefing will usually be followed by a more full explanation of HOW to do whatever is being taught; WHEN to do it; and, particularly, WHY it is important for the content to be taught in a certain way.

Communicating information of this nature plays a vital part in the normal skill training technique of EXPLANATION, DEMONSTRATION and PRACTICE which will be covered in detail in section 4.7.

Care must be taken not to 'overload' the pupil. Information should be divided into the following categories:

> MUST KNOW;
> SHOULD KNOW;
> COULD KNOW.

The instructor should identify the 'key points' of the message and then concentrate on making sure that the pupil understands these MUST KNOW elements. Further information from the SHOULD KNOW and COULD KNOW categories may be given in response to questions from the pupil or filled in later, possibly on the move as situations develop which require this further information to be given.

Making sure that the pupil knows and understands everything that he needs to know can be achieved by:

- breaking the information down into its component parts;
- using mnemonics to make routines more memorable – for example, MSM, PSL and LAD;
- using word associations like 'Creep and Peep';
- using visual keys like 'Think of the thickness of a coin';
- slowing or quickening the speed of your speech to match the speed at which you want the action to be carried out;
- using pauses after important points have been made;
- using the Q/A technique after each key point has been made to confirm their understanding of what has been said; and

- using visual aids where appropriate and, if the subject is technical, giving hand-outs to the pupil to refer to after the lesson.

At the end of each lesson which has contained a briefing or a full explanation, assess your own performance. Ask yourself 'Has the pupil understood all the key points which I have explained?'

3.4

GIVING INSTRUCTIONS AND DIRECTIONS

Problems will arise during driving lessons if the instructions and directions given by the instructor are not given in a clear and unmistakable manner. You need to take account of all the previous points made about verbal communication but you should also take special note of the following:

- Use language that will be understood by the pupil to avoid any confusion arising.
- Avoid ambiguous words which might be misinterpreted by the pupil. For example: 'Right', meaning OK or correct, could cause the pupil to think you want them to turn right; 'top', meaning top gear, could be misheard as 'stop', especially on a hot day with all the windows down and noise from traffic.
- When on the move give the instruction and directions early enough for the pupil to do whatever is necessary without rushing.
- Match the level of the instruction to the ability of the pupil. A novice will need almost total instruction in what to do, whereas a trained pupil may only need the occasional 'key-word' prompt.
- Use the ALERT–DIRECT–IDENTIFY routine. For example: 'I would like you to' (ALERT) '. . . take the next road on the left please' (DIRECT) 'It's just around the bend' (IDENTIFY).

Never forget that less experienced pupils will take longer to react to the instruction or direction. An instruction given too late is likely to result in the pupil:

- missing out important looking;
- losing control with feet or hands;

- assessing situations incorrectly;
- making poor decisions; and
- losing confidence.

When teaching a pupil who is at an advanced stage, you should transfer the responsibility of working out where the various junctions and hazards are by not giving the pupil too much help. For many pupils the driving test will be the first opportunity that they have to drive on their own without your help.

A very good way of transferring responsibility and finding out whether the pupil is ready to drive unaccompanied would be to say ten minutes before the end of the lesson: 'Do you think you could find your way back home from here on your own?' If the answer is yes, then let the pupil drive back without any instructions or directions being given.

Once his pupil is coming up to test standard, the instructor should use phraseology similar to that of the examiner as a way of preparing the pupil for the testing situation. It is extremely important that instructors sit in the back on at least one test every six months so that they can re-affirm their understanding of how the examiner gives his instructions and the timing of them.

One of the most common criticisms of instructors is that of over-instruction. This happens because the instructor does not know when to 'drop out'. Are you guilty of 'over-instructing'? If so, what are you going to do about it?

At the end of each lesson you will need to ask yourself:

- Were the instructions and directions given to my pupil in a clear and unmistakable manner?
- Did the timing of the directions given allow the pupil to do all the things necessary to deal with the situation?
- Was there any ambiguity in the instructions and directions given?

3.5

USING POSITIVE BODY LANGUAGE

Whenever we communicate with others, we use body language – it is unavoidable and instinctive. Speech and the development of language began about 500,000 years ago but it is probable that body language has been used for at least one million years.

Because body language is so deeply ingrained in us, it is difficult to disguise and even when you are not speaking you are sending messages to others, sometimes without even being aware of it. Your physical appearance, posture, gestures, gaze and facial expressions indicate to others your moods and feelings.

> *It is important for driving instructors to be able to use positive body language and interpret the body language of their learners.*

Because the body language of your learners may give you more information about their mood and receptiveness than what they are saying, being able to interpret accurately these silent signals will assist you in deciding whether to modify your delivery, back off, or even change the activity entirely. For example, should the face of your pupil show frustration when failing to master a reversing exercise, you may decide to switch to something that is less demanding in order to boost their confidence rather than destroy it.

The ability to interpret body language will also enable you to tell whether there is any difference between what the pupil is saying and what they really think. The driving instructor needs to develop a high degree of perceptual sensitivity to be able to read accurately the silent signals being sent by his pupils.

Body language is particularly important in interviewing, negotiating, selling and buying situations. Although the general rules regarding body language will apply at meetings, in the classroom or during social encounters, when you are giving driving lessons your skills will need to be adapted to take account of the fact that, on the move, you can only see the side of your pupil's face. (We do not encourage our pupils to look at us while they are driving!) Of course, while stationary you will often be able to see their eyes as well.

If you want to be able to use your own body language in a positive way and be able to read that of others, you need to recognise the constituents of body language. There are seven main constituents, some of which are more relevant to driving instruction than others:

- FACIAL EXPRESSIONS;
- GAZE;

- POSTURE;
- GESTURES;
- PROXIMITY;
- TOUCH; and
- PERSONAL APPEARANCE.

When teaching in the car, the instructor needs to spend much time not only reading the road ahead but looking at the face, eyes, hands and feet of his pupils. Although the hands and feet will tell how well the controls are being used, the face and eyes will not only show where the pupil is looking but also what they may be thinking or feeling.

FACIAL EXPRESSIONS

In driving instruction facial expressions are most useful to the instructor. The face is highly visible (even in profile) and is capable of conveying one's innermost feelings. Think of the expression on the face of someone who has just failed the driving test and then compare it with that of someone else who has just passed!

The face is a very spontaneous communicator of messages and will generally convey the feelings of its owner in a uniform way. The face is, therefore, a fairly reliable indicator of happiness or despair, pain or pleasure. Consequently, when teaching, you should ensure that your facial expressions do not contradict what you are saying – if they do, it will have a disturbing effect on your pupils.

GAZE

When explaining things to your pupil, or debriefing at the side of the road, or in a classroom situation, you will normally have eye-to-eye contact. The eyes can tell you a great deal about what people may be feeling but, with skill and practice, your eyes can tell others what you want them to think you are feeling. Poker players and salesmen use this technique to good effect, sometimes with high stakes to play for.

A strong gaze usually shows that you are being attentive and concentrating on what the other person is saying. However, in some cultures it is not deemed polite to stare. When people become embarrassed they will often break eye contact and look away.

Breaking eye contact may show that you have made an error or cannot answer a question, while a reluctance to look at someone at all may show your dislike or distrust of that person.

However, establishing strong eye contact will show that you have a genuine desire to communicate and will be seen by your pupils as an invitation to speak. It is a cultural expectation, especially of women, that people look at each other when communicating. If you are reluctant to look someone in the face when talking to them, or continually shift your eyes around, you will not inspire trust.

Your emotions, attitudes and honesty, as portrayed by your eye contact, make gaze an important constituent of your body language. Aggressive stares and shifty looks should be avoided. You should try to develop a strong gaze, with an occasional blink or look away which will make people feel more comfortable and receptive.

POSTURE

In the confined space of a motor car, when your feet and hands are occupied, posture is not quite so revealing as in a classroom situation where how you stand or sit and the position of your arms and legs will reflect your feelings and attitudes to others.

A normal seating position which allows the pupil to reach the foot and hand controls comfortably will of course determine the 'angles' of their legs and arms.

You can display a warmth and liking for someone by leaning towards them slightly, with your arms relaxed. You can show your disgust at their actions by turning away and looking out of the window. You must be careful not to hover over the dual controls with your feet as this will unnerve the pupil and destroy their self-confidence. You should avoid continually looking round to check the blindspots on the move for the same reason. Careful and subtle use of the mirrors will achieve the same objective but without worrying the pupil.

In meetings or in the classroom, your posture becomes much more important. An erect posture will indicate a sense of pride, confidence and self-discipline, while stooping shoulders and head down may be interpreted as being slovenly or lacking in confidence. Your impressions of others and their impressions of you will be influenced by posture and gait. When walking across the room, you should therefore adopt a confident purposeful walk, which will indicate self-assurance, confidence and personal dynamism.

When giving presentations, you can use posture and body movements to help to bring your story to life, supporting any verbal message, thus maintaining the interest of those watching and listening.

GESTURES

Gestures may occasionally be used instead of words in certain circumstances. If you are trying to communicate with a deaf person or someone who does not speak English, gestures will help you to communicate. Your hands can be used to demonstrate how the clutch plates come together, for example.

A nod of the head, or a wave of the hand are friendly, passive signals which may be given to other instructors or road-users to acknowledge a courtesy whereas a shaking of the fist conveys aggression. Sometimes your gestures will be involuntary. For example, scratching your head or chin may signal that you are uneasy or concerned about what your pupil is doing. The driving instructor who continually fidgets or waves his arms about will give his pupil the impression that he is nervous or worried. This will do little to build up the pupil's confidence! Gesticulations of this nature or pen waving while going along the road will also distract the pupil from concentrating on the road and could be dangerous.

To control them, you need to be aware of your gestures, especially those that may be distracting to others. If you give presentations at meetings or in the classroom, a videotape of your performance will be invaluable in helping you to recognise those gestures that are weak and those that are effective in emphasising and reinforcing your verbal messages. If you are uncomfortable using deliberately planned gestures, rehearsal and practice will allow you to deliver them in such a way that they appear to be spontaneous and natural rather than forced and awkward.

PROXIMITY (PERSONAL SPACE)

The driving instructor should be aware that each pupil needs a certain amount of personal space (a 'space bubble') with which they feel comfortable. Encroaching on this personal space may make the pupil feel uncomfortable, and could even cause him change to a different driving instructor.

Instructors need to ensure that this space is not so great that their teaching loses its effectiveness. The diagram below shows the different environments and situations and the amount of space required.

ENVIRONMENT   **SPACE REQUIRED**

In the car A few inches

With lovers, close
friends and relatives,   About 18 inches
spouses and children   or 45 cms

Social functions  About 45 to 120 cms

In the classroom   Public space of
with strangers      between 120 cms
or at business   and 3 metres
meetings

When giving a   Lecturer space
lecture or      of at least
talking at a   3 metres
conference

The space bubble

You will see from the diagram that the driving instructor is in the privileged position of being allowed to get closer than everybody else, with the exception perhaps of the family doctor!

The amount of personal space required is sometimes dependent on the cultural background of the person. In many Mediterranean countries and in Norway, for example, people feel comfortable almost rubbing shoulders. For most English people this would be quite unacceptable.

You will need to be very sensitive to the needs of each individual pupil in this respect and generally should avoid getting too close wherever possible. This can be difficult in a small car, especially if both you and the pupil are quite large!

In the classroom, distance can be a barrier to communication, as can speaking from behind a desk, or up on a rostrum. Avoid being seen as authoritarian and try to establish an informal atmosphere. For instance, it can sometimes be more effective to sit on the edge of the desk than behind it.

Sometimes you may wish to maintain a physical barrier between you and whoever you are talking to. If you are reprimanding one of your instructors for being late, for example, you may wish to reinforce your authority by sitting behind a desk. Similarly a female secretary might feel threatened if her male boss sits too close to her while dictating a letter. In this case a physical barrier would be appropriate.

TOUCH

Formal touches are important when meeting someone for the first time, like a new pupil. A firm (but not crushing) handshake will indicate self-confidence which is especially important when a male meets another male. A limp, handshake implies weakness and it would be better not to give one at all.

At the end of a lesson a handshake is not really necessary and a wave or pat on the back might be more effective. These can also be nice gestures when the pupil passes the driving test.

You must be extremely careful not to touch pupils in the car unless it is for reasons of safety. Touching pupils may make them feel uncomfortable or threatened and cause them to distrust your motives. Pupils often change instructors because unnecessary physical contact upset them.

Cultural backgrounds sometimes influence the desire to touch and be touched. For example, people from the Greek island of Rhodes continually touch each other during conversation so, if you have a pupil from this lovely island, watch out!

If a pupil has just received some distressing news you might feel tempted to give them a hug but, generally, a sympathetic ear is just as effective and certainly less likely to be misinterpreted as a social advance.

PERSONAL APPEARANCE

When you are a driving instructor, from the moment you leave home to the moment you return back at the end of the day, you are under scrutiny from the public, particularly if you have your name on the car! Your appearance, dress and grooming may create an initial impression that is very difficult to change.

When considering body language, your personal appearance, hair and the clothes that you wear are of great importance because you may well have more control over them than your facial features and posture. There is little we can do to change our shape, features and size, but much can be done to improve our appearance, the suitability of our clothes and the general impression that we convey.

When teaching people to drive, you do of course have to take account of the weather conditions and, while it might not be necessary to wear a three-piece suit, you can still dress casually but smartly. In the summer and winter you will need to dress for comfort, but never forget that your appearance can influence your impact on people and can help to create a favourable or an unfavourable impression.

Propriety of dress is particularly important for the female instructor to help overcome possible problems with male pupils who might see revealing clothes, together with the natural caring attitude of the teacher, as an invitation to develop social relationships.

3.6

INTERPRETING THE BODY LANGUAGE OF THE LEARNER

All the constituents of body language that we have discussed in the previous section may combine to present a positive image to those you come into contact with.

It is equally important that you recognise the silent signals your pupils give out. We have chosen common signs that your pupils may give you to indicate the way they feel. However, every pupil is an individual and things are very rarely black and white.

Never forget that if you want to teach John how to drive, you have first got to know all about driving, but you have also got to know all about John! Getting to know your pupils better will assist you in accurately interpreting their body language. Generally speaking, the following rules apply.

A learner who is willing to listen:

- sits with his head on one side;
- looks directly at you;
- rests his chin on the palm of his hand;
- nods in agreement with what is being said;
- says things like 'I see'.

A learner who is pleased:

- smiles;
- uses strong eye contact;
- can't stop talking;
- uses humour in his speech;
- is polite and courteous.

A learner who is anxious to ask a question:

- lifts his hand or finger up;
- shifts his sitting position;
- fidgets with his ear or chin;
- looks intently at you with his head on one side.

A learner who is annoyed with himself:

- shakes his head;
- tightly crosses his arms;
- hits the steering wheel;
- exhales loudly;
- frowns.

A learner who has had a fright:

- covers his eyes up with his hands;
- opens his mouth and puts his head back;
- bites his bottom lip;
- becomes red in the face;
- inhales sharply.

A learner who is disappointed:

- frowns or scowls;
- drops his shoulders and lets his head drop forwards;
- lets his arms fall into his lap;
- droops his mouth.

A learner who is nervous:

- talks incessantly about nothing;
- tightens his grip on the steering wheel;
- licks his lips;
- bites his nails or chews his fingers.

Looking at your pupils will not only allow you to see and interpret their body language, but also assist you in identifying faults being made which involve their feet, hands and eyes. If you do not see the fault, how can you suggest a remedy for it?

3.7

LISTENING SKILLS

We have two ears but only one mouth and we should use them in those proportions. We will learn more about our learner's needs by asking questions and listening to what they say than we will by talking.

You need to pay particular attention to anything that your pupil says voluntarily and try to look at them when they are talking so that you can pick up the silent signals as well. These non-verbal messages will often reinforce the verbal message and help you to understand what the person is really feeling. This may often be at variance with what they are saying.

You can then use questions like 'You don't seem too happy with that. Is there anything that you don't understand?'

When people are listening, they tend to show their interest and attention both verbally and non-verbally. They will nod their heads, lean forward, and say things like 'Yes, I see', 'That's true', 'I absolutely agree' and 'Hear, hear'.

On the other hand, if they are not listening, they do not look at you, they stare out of the window, yawn or even fall asleep. Any of these responses should tell you quite explicitly that they are bored.

You can develop your listening skills in the following ways:

- 'Listen' with your eyes as well as your ears. By looking at the speaker you will not only hear the words but detect the silent signals which help you to understand the *true* meaning of what the person is saying;
- Ask questions. If anything is unclear, do not be afraid of asking for it to be clarified, and if you disagree with the point being made, then say so, but give your reasons why.

Use open-ended questions to test people's understanding of anything you have explained to them and seek their views and opinions on what you are saying. When they respond, hear them out; do not interrupt – wait until they have finished speaking before replying.

The communication skills of both speaking and listening will help you in presenting a driving lesson and making presentations to larger groups. Classroom skills are covered in section 4.13.

Every lesson that you give is an opportunity to practice your skills as a communicator. At the end of each lesson, you should analyse your own performance with a view to improving your ability. Ask yourself:

- Have I spent enough time looking at and listening to my pupil?
- Have I misinterpreted or not seen any silent signals?
- Have I missed faults of control or observational errors made by my pupil due to not looking at them enough?
- Has my own body language been positive or have I put the pupil off by the way in which I have reacted to their actions and responses to my questions?
- Could I have communicated with my pupil more effectively today?

4

Specialist Skills for Driving Instructors

Many qualified drivers seem to think that just because they can drive this automatically qualifies them to be able to teach someone else how to drive. When they hear that a friend is taking lessons they will often say 'I'll give you some lessons if you like'.

Another common statement one hears from qualified drivers is 'I only had six lessons and passed the test first time!'. Of course, it is possible to teach somebody how to handle the controls of a vehicle in a few hours. The modern motor car is much easier to drive than its predecessors. Gone is the need to double de-clutch, use the gears to help slow down and grapple with poor steering, bad suspension and deficient tyres.

What has changed, however, is the density of traffic and the amount of space available. Learner drivers today face an increasingly complex set of problems when dealing with the speed and density of modern day traffic.

The driving instruction industry needs to change people's attitudes, making the general public aware that driving today requires specialist skills, and specialist teachers to teach those skills.

> *Traditional 'hit and miss' teaching methods are inadequate in today's driving environment.*

The modern day instructor has had to adapt and change in order to prepare learner drivers for a lifetime of safe driving.

Although driving instructors are 'teachers of driving', they have to use specialist skills which go far beyond teaching practices generally. This chapter covers some of those 'specialist skills'.

4.1

TEACHING BY OBJECTIVES

The theory of teaching by objectives is covered in detail in *The Driving Instructor's Handbook*. In this section of the book, we will be explaining how to put the theory into practice, using your PTS. General objectives give the teaching goals. These need to be broken down into more specific objectives which allow the pupil to demonstrate his attainment of those goals.

In section 2.5 we have already covered: learning to memorise something; learning to understand something; learning to do something; and attitude development. When teaching someone how to drive, it is not very helpful to separate these activities. The learner needs to practise all of the above, and then reflect on the experience with guidance from the instructor.

Driving instructors are rather like baby-sitters. They spend time with their charges for perhaps only one or two hours a week. As soon as the children they are looking after can fend for themselves, the baby-sitter is no longer required. Once learner drivers have passed the L test, they have no further need for their driving instructors and will possibly never see them again unless they are persuaded to take some motorway lessons or preparation for an advanced test.

You may recall the first time your own children, having just passed the L test, informed you that they were going to drive to some far distant place, where they had never been before. You will have felt worried and concerned about them making the trip, but all you could do about it was to make sure that they knew where they were going and how they were going to get there.

You would then have anxiously waited, hoping that they didn't encounter too many problems on the way, solved whatever problems they did meet, in the way that you had taught them to, and made sensible decisions based on safety. When they returned home safely, you probably breathed a sigh of relief.

Given the limitations of time and money, all we can hope to achieve when teaching our learners is that they know 'where they are going, and how they are going to get there'.

There will probably be big gaps in their knowledge, understanding, skills and their attitude may need modifying from time to time. They will undoubtedly take risks along the way, but, hopefully, they will learn from the experience.

So, faced with this problem, how can we make the best use of the short amount of time available for teaching? We need to ask ourselves:

- What are our pupils setting out to achieve?
- What is the best way of helping them to achieve it in the time available?

If we are absolutely honest with ourselves, the answers to these questions will probably be 'pass the L test' and 'plan a course of lessons linked to the requirements of the test'.

Until the driving instruction industry gets its act together and starts changing the public's perception of how many lessons people should have, how much they should be prepared to spend on driving lessons and that safe driving for life should be the main objective, rather than passing the L test, it is going to be left to the individual instructor to use his selling skills. He needs to persuade his learners that the test is just an entrance examination and not a degree course. Pupils should be encouraged to take motorway lessons, advanced driving courses, better driving courses etc.

Whatever the type of course or subject matter, the objectives for each particular pupil will need to be clearly defined and stated.

When teaching by objectives, Bloom's three main categories of learning – AFFECTIVE DOMAIN, COGNITIVE DOMAIN and PSYCHO-MOTOR DOMAIN (see section 2.5) – will probably play a part in deciding the mode of the instruction to be given.

Teaching by objectives, or using a 'stepping-stone' approach, will make the learning process more enjoyable for the learner in that he will be able to see and measure how his skill is progressing against the requirements of the L test.

One of the biggest problems for learners when they first start their lessons is that they have a feeling of insecurity – this is due largely to them not being able to compare their progress, or lack of it, with that of their peers, who may also be learning to drive.

Using a stepping-stone approach leading up to the test does help to overcome this problem. When they have achieved one objective, then they move on to the next one, and so on. If they are unable to achieve an objective, then this is where your skill as a teacher is put to the test. You will have to find the right method for your pupil – one which ensures that he learns. Knowing when to encourage, praise, question, explain, demonstrate and assess are the skills of the teacher.

It is essential to remember that there is no such thing as a bad learner. The inability of the pupil to learn is much more likely to be the fault of the teacher! Your skill will be to set the objectives for the pupil just at the correct level, so as to give him a realistic target to aim for. When he hits that target, he should feel a sense of achievement which will stimulate him to want to make more progress.

The most important factor in the selection of the objectives is that both the instructor and the pupil agree what they are to be, and that some record is kept of progress made. Using this system gives an immediate progress chart for each pupil and also acts as a memory prompt for the instructor so that he can remember which particular item is the next one to be covered during the lessons.

It is also helpful if pupils might be switched from one instructor to another for any reason, such as in the event of illness or holidays, or even moving away to another area.

By using a progress chart similar to that shown opposite, a replacement instructor can pick up where the previous instructor has left off.

Name......................

Subject	DATE Talk through	DATE Prompted	DATE Unaided
Starting precautions			
Make proper use of: accelerator clutch gears footbrake handbrake steering			
Move off safely			
Emergency stop			
Reverse left			
Reverse right			
Turn in the road			
Reverse park			
Use of mirrors			
Use of signals			
Act on signs/signals			
Making progress			
T Junctions: M S M speed on approach observations position/right position/left			
Crossroads: M S M speed on approach observations position/right position/left position/ahead			
Roundabouts: M S M speed on approach observations position/left position/ahead position/right			
Meet others			
Safety clearances			
Crossing path of others			
Pedestrian crossings			
Overtaking			
Dual carriageways			
Railway crossings			
Parking			
Anticipating: pedestrians cyclists other drivers			

Sample progress chart

As well as giving each pupil a copy of their progress chart on a record or appointment card, the instructor should also keep a master list in the car so that each pupil's progress can be monitored. Progress sheets can be filed on a clip board in alphabetical order by surname.

Do not lose sight of the fact that although we may be giving the pupil a 'test related' programme of learning, we are also preparing him for a lifetime of safe driving. The requirements of the test go further than performing the set exercises. Knowledge, understanding and attitude all come into it as well as practical skill. Your course of instruction should cover all of these.

In using objectives based on the L test, all we have given our learners is a firm foundation. Drivers will reflect on their performance long after they have passed the driving test. There will undoubtedly be gaps which are likely to be filled as they gain experience.

The LEARNING CIRCLE of learning, practice and reflection which we saw in section 2.3 will hold good for the rest of their driving lives!

When teaching by objectives you will need to ask yourself at the end of each lesson:

- Have I set the objectives at a realistic level for the pupil?
- Am I concentrating too much on 'getting them through the test' instead of teaching them safe driving for life?
- Am I paying enough attention to knowledge, understanding and attitude, or spending too much time on skill training?
- Have I kept each pupil's progress chart up to date?
- Have I kept my own progress chart for each pupil up to date?

4.2

LESSON PLANNING

This section will show you how to plan a driving lesson to suit the needs of each individual pupil.

> *You should start each lesson with a clear idea of* WHAT *you are going to teach and* WHY *you are going to teach it,* WHERE *the lesson is going to take place,* HOW *the time available is to be utilised and* HOW *the lesson is going to be structured.*

At the start of a check test, the examiner will often ask the instructor 'What is your lesson plan for today?'. It is not unusual for the reply to be 'Well, I just thought we would drive around for a bit and see how things develop'!

Professional driving instruction should not be a matter of driving around for a bit to see what develops. The good instructor should:

- have a clearly defined plan of what is going to be taught;
- take into account the level of ability of the pupil when setting the objectives for the lesson to be given; and
- know in advance what activities are going to take place during the lesson and how the pupil is going to be kept interested and attentive.

A grade six instructor will probably go a lot further than that. He would be likely to:

- have specified learning goals for the student;
- vary the teaching methods to suit those goals and the characteristics of the student;
- demonstrate a range of skills when using these teaching methods and any visual or learning aids;
- carefully manage the time, structure and content of the lesson;
- adapt the lesson to suit the perceived needs of the student where necessary;
- identify, analyse and correct faults;
- identify any problem areas, taking remedial action or recommending further training where necessary;
- comply with DSA examination requirements when appropriate;
- take account of the safety of the student, the passenger and any other road-users at all times;
- offer feedback to the student during and at the end of the lesson where appropriate;
- link forward to the next lesson; and
- evaluate what learning has taken place.

Lesson planning for the classroom environment is slightly different and is covered in section 4.13.

When teaching in the car, many instructors will have a structured lesson plan. Of course, this may need to be changed if problems are encountered as the lesson progresses. For example, you might plan to teach the pupil how to carry out one of the manoeuvres but, on the way to a suitable place, the pupil fails to see a pedestrian who is just about to step onto a pedestrian crossing. This causes you to have to use the dual controls.

In view of the seriousness of the error, it would make sense to postpone the original manoeuvre planned and spend some time on dealing with how to approach pedestrian crossings, stopping when necessary.

This should not present any problems for the learner as long as he is told why the lesson plan has been changed, and that the original subject will be covered in a future lesson.

The following is an example of a formal lesson plan.

LESSON PLAN

Partly trained pupil

Instruction in turning the car round to face the opposite way using forward and reverse gears.

Objectives

By the end of the lesson the pupil will be able to:

1) Choose an appropriate site for the manoeuvre
2) Co-ordinate the controls with reasonable smoothness
3) Take effective observation before and during the manoeuvre
4) Carry out the manoeuvre with reasonable accuracy

TIME	MAIN POINTS AND METHOD	TEACHING AIDS
4–8 minutes approx	Q/A recap and briefing: explanation of manoeuvre	'DRIVING' diagram
5–10 minutes approx	Demonstration and complete talk-through practice	
5 minutes approx	Debriefing, feedback, encouragement, praise, fault analysis	'DRIVING' diagram if appropriate
5–10 minutes approx	Remedial practice; prompts if necessary	
5 minutes	Debriefing, feedback, encouragement, praise, fault analysis, link forward to next lesson	

Please note that in the lesson plan shown above, the timings are only a guide and will vary depending on the pupil's knowledge, response and receptiveness.

Taking account of the individual needs of the pupil, the lesson plan will also need to be linked in with:

• matching the level of instruction to the ability of the pupil; and
• route selection and planning.

These items are covered separately in sections 4.3 and 4.4, but they form an integral part of any lesson plan.

To appreciate the extent of the task that faces you, consider how you would plan a lesson for each of the potential pupils listed below

– what type of routes you would choose and how you would vary your level of instruction.

- An absolute beginner.
- A partly trained pupil.
- A pupil at about L test standard.
- Somebody who has recently passed the L test but has never driven on motorways.
- Somebody who passed the L test a few years ago but has not driven since.
- A full licence holder who wishes to take the IAM or RoSPA advanced test.
- A company driver taking a 'defensive driving' course.
- The holder of a full foreign licence who has never driven in this country or on the left-hand side of the road.
- Somebody who is just about to appear in court on a traffic offence and wishes to take a course as part of his 'mitigating circumstances'.
- Somebody who has to take an ordinary length test as part of a court order.
- Somebody who has to take an extended test as part of a court order.

When you have read sections 4.3 and 4.4, come back to the notes you have made regarding your lesson plans for the different types of pupils and see whether you would need to change anything!

At the end of each driving lesson, you should ask yourself:

- Did the lesson plan help the student to achieve the objectives stated at the beginning of the lesson?
- Did I involve the pupil in the lesson sufficiently?
- Should I have changed the lesson plan to take account of perceived problems?
- Did I give the pupil enough feedback on how well he was doing?
- Were the lesson plan; routes chosen; and level of instruction given, 'right' for the pupil?
- With hindsight, was there anything I should have done differently?

4.3

MATCHING THE LEVEL OF INSTRUCTION TO THE ABILITY OF THE PUPIL

In most driving lessons, the professional instructor will be involved in the following activities:

- teaching new skills;
- consolidating partly learnt skills; and
- assessing skills already learnt or partly learnt.

Some lessons may contain a mixture of all three elements or two of the three. Many instructors make the mistake of trying to cram too many activities into the one lesson to the detriment of the learning process.

As well as planning the content of the lesson to be given, the instructor needs carefully to consider the routes and areas chosen and the level of instruction required for each particular pupil.

One of the problems for instructors is knowing when to 'drop out' and transfer to the pupil the responsibility for solving problems and making decisions. The sooner the learner starts to think things out and make decisions for himself, the sooner he will be ready to drive unaccompanied.

For many learners, the first time they ever drive 'unaccompanied' will be on the L test, when the examiner is there purely as an observer.

The skilful instructor knows when to shut up. Of course, in most driving lessons, you will need to give directions but, during the lessons immediately before the test, it would be very beneficial to the learner if you say 'Let's see if you can drive home on your own, without me saying anything at all. You make all the decisions and pretend that I am not here.' You would, of course, need to be sure that your pupil knew the way home.

In this situation, the only time the instructor should intervene is for safety reasons. This exercise will boost the confidence of the pupil coming up to the test, and also give the instructor a measure of the pupil's readiness to drive unaccompanied. At the end of the 'unaccompanied drive' it will be useful to the instructor to ask the pupil: 'How did you feel about driving on your own then?'

Some feedback would then need to be given to the pupil. A requirement for more lessons might be necessary.

Two very common instructional errors arise from the instructor not matching the level of instruction to suit the level of ability of the pupil.

OVER-INSTRUCTION

This often occurs when the instructor is teaching a new skill, or who has identified a problem area, and is giving the pupil a complete 'talk-through' on the subject being covered. The new skill will probably be mixed in with skills which are already learnt or partly learnt.

For example, the instructor may be talking the pupil through a difficult junction, with the added problem of road-works. When the junction has been negotiated, he asks the pupil to pull in and park somewhere convenient, so that he can discuss what happened, forgets that the pupil knows how to park unaccompanied and says: 'Gently brake to slow; clutch down; gently brake to stop; apply the handbrake; select neutral'.

The pupil may have parked a hundred times unaccompanied, without any problem. What has happened is that the instructor has got so involved in the 'talk-through' mode, that he has forgotten when to shut up!

You should therefore try to restrict your prompted practice or talk-through to those aspects of driving which are new to the pupil, or which are as yet unaccomplished. Over-instruction is particularly common when the pupil is approaching test standard. It is as if the instructor is reluctant to 'let go of the reins'. Always remember that at this level the pupil will learn a lot more by doing it himself, even if he gets it wrong, than by listening to you telling him what to do.

UNDER-INSTRUCTION

This is particularly common when the pupil is in the novice stage or is only partially trained. When teaching new skills you need to control the practice so that, where possible, the pupil gets it right first time. There is nothing more motivating for the pupil than success, even though that success may be the result of you prompting or talking the pupil through the task. Your function is to talk the pupils through each stage of the operation, skill or exercise until they develop the ability and confidence to do it for themselves.

The need for a full-talk through is greatest in the early stages of learning a particular task so as to lessen the risk of vehicle abuse and inconvenience or danger to other road-users.

The talk-through must give the pupil enough time to interpret and execute your instructions comfortably. The speed with which each pupil will be able to do this is likely to vary. You therefore need to match the level of instruction and the timing of your delivery to the particular needs of the pupil.

Knowing when to drop out is important. If you leave the pupil on his own too soon, resulting in a poor execution of the task, it can be very demotivating. However, when you consider the pupil is ready to take personal responsibility for his actions you should encourage him to do so. Some pupils will need lots of encouragement to act and think for themselves. Others will make rapid progress when left to work on their own initiative.

You might need to change from 'talk-through' mode to 'prompted practice' mode. Prompting is the natural progression from controlled practice and will largely depend on the ability and willingness of the pupil to make decisions for himself.

If conditions become too busy for the pupil's ability or potential danger is a factor, then the pupil may be reluctant to make any decisions at all. Where these situations arise you must be prepared to step in and prompt when required.

The use of detailed instructions should decrease as the ability of the pupil increases, thereby transferring the responsibility for making decisions and acting on them from you to the pupil.

In the last few lessons leading up to the driving test, it should not be necessary for you to prompt the pupil at all. If this is not the case, then you have a selling job to do. You need to either sell more lessons and the necessity for further practice or postponement of the test.

At the end of each lesson ask yourself:

- Did I match the level of the instruction given to the ability of the pupil?
- Did I over-instruct on things which the pupil should need no instruction on?
- Did I leave the pupil to do things on his own, when I should have been prompting?

4.4

ROUTE PLANNING

Route selection and planning is itself a Practical Teaching Skill and is an essential part of lesson preparation and planning. Part of an instructor's role is to create a situation in which learning can take place, and the selection of routes is an integral element in this process.

The ideal route would be one that takes account of the character and level of ability of the pupil. It should be designed to stretch them but not be daunting.

Using training routes which are not relevant to the needs of the pupil or not appropriate to the requirements of the lesson plan can have an extremely negative effect on the training.

The confidence of some learners is destroyed because they are taken into difficult situations which require good clutch control before they have mastered this skill. Imagine how you would feel if you were sitting at a red traffic light on your first driving lesson and you stalled the engine a couple of times!

If a new driver is unnecessarily exposed to road and traffic conditions with which they are unable to cope, it is quite likely that the amount of learning taking place will be reduced. In the most extreme case, the pupil's confidence will be severely affected, with a detrimental effect on learning or even a reversal of the learning process.

At the other end of the scale, restricting the experienced learner to inappropriate basic routes will not encourage them to develop their skills.

When planning routes, you should consider some of the main requirements:

- the specific objectives for the lesson;
- the standard and ability of the pupil combined with the need to introduce or improve any skill or procedure;
- any particular weaknesses or strengths of the pupil;
- any hazards or features which you may want to include or avoid in the overall lesson plan;
- the length of time available for the lesson;
- whether any danger or inconvenience might be caused by using a particular area at a particular time: and

- if any unnecessary or excessive nuisance would be caused to local residents.

Ideally, you should have a thorough knowledge of the training area and any local traffic conditions. However, this is not always practicable or possible, and care will need to be taken to avoid any extreme conditions.

If, because of the local geography and the limited time available, complicated situations cannot be avoided, consider whether you should drive the pupil to a more appropriate training area. In this event, use the drive to give a demonstration of any relevant points and to include a 'talk-through' of what you are doing.

Training routes and areas tend to fall into three main categories – nursery or basic, intermediate and advanced. There will not be a clear division between the three groups and there will often be a considerable overlap from one group to another. Nevertheless, it is important that you have a clear idea of the appropriate routes within your own working environment.

Nursery Routes – These will normally include fairly long, straight, wide roads without too many parked vehicles and avoid pedestrian crossings, traffic lights or roundabouts. This type of route will incorporate progressively most or all of the following features:

- roads which are long enough to allow for a reasonable progression through all the gears and for stopping from various speeds;
- several upward and downward gradients suitable for starting and stopping;
- left- and right-hand bends to develop speed adjustment and gear changing skills
- left turns from main roads to side roads;
- left turns from side roads to main roads; and
- right turns into side roads and onto main roads.

Intermediate Routes – These should include busier junctions and general traffic conditions. At this stage, try to avoid dual carriageways, multi-lane roads and any one-way systems. Some, or all of the following features might be incorporated in the routes:

- crossroads and junctions with 'stop' and 'give way' signs;
- several uphill give-way junctions:
- traffic lights and basic roundabouts; and
- areas for manoeuvring.

Care should be taken to avoid too many complicated traffic situations – for example, right turns onto exceptionally busy main roads or complex junctions.

Advanced Routes – These will incorporate most of the features of the intermediate routes and should be extended to give a wider variety of traffic and road conditions. They should include, where possible, dual carriageways, multi-lane roads and one-way systems as well as residential, urban and rural roads. A properly planned 'advanced' route will provide the opportunity to conduct mock tests without using actual test routes. You should be able to find routes that include:

- different types of pedestrian crossings;
- roads with varying speed limits;
- level crossings, dual carriageways and one-way streets;
- multi-laned roads for lane selection and lane discipline; and
- rural, urban and residential roads

Starting with nursery routes, try to introduce new elements and situations at a controlled rate bearing in mind the needs of the pupils and the level of their ability. Get used to what seems to be 'their own pace' – one at which they feel comfortable.

There may be occasions when a mixture of all types of route may be incorporated into one lesson – for example, when making an initial assessment of a new pupil who has previous driving experience.

Ideally, you should start off with a fairly wide selection of routes. This will give you the opportunity to vary and extend them with experience. Retain a certain amount of flexibility in using the planned routes because you may, for instance, need to spend more time than anticipated on a topic which the pupil is finding more difficult than expected.

If a specific problem is identified, you may need to demonstrate or contrive to bring the pupil back to a particular junction in order to 'recreate' a situation.

Excessive repetition of identical routes will often lead to a lack of interest or response from the pupil. This in turn will lead to slow progress in learning and may also be counterproductive. Some variation of routes is essential to the learning process and will sustain the pupil's interest and motivation. Occasionally, however, you may decide that a certain amount of repetition is necessary to work on a specific task relevant to the objectives for a particular lesson.

Remember that training routes are often a compromise between the ideal and the reality of local conditions in the training area. The nature of traffic conditions can vary enormously from time to time and from lesson to lesson. You may find that a carefully planned route may unexpectedly prove unsuitable and your pupil is faced with a situation that he is not ready for. Careful route planning can, however, keep these incidents to a manageable level. Be ready to extend the length of a lesson for a particular pupil if appropriate training routes are not readily available in the immediate vicinity.

At the end of each lesson, ask yourself:

- Did I choose a route that was suitable for the level of ability of the pupil and the objectives stated?
- Did I vary the route sufficiently to sustain the interest of the pupil?
- Am I using routes which stretch the ability of the pupil but without destroying their confidence?

4.5

FAULT ASSESSMENT

This section will assist you in assessing the faults made by your pupils. Assessment will be purely visual and relate to driver errors which will be:

IN-CAR (Errors of control)
OUTSIDE THE CAR (Errors of road procedure)

You will often find that errors made in the car will lead to errors of road procedure, lack of accuracy, or failure to respond correctly to external traffic situations.

You will need to use your eyes, dividing your attention between what is happening on the road ahead, what is happening behind and what your pupil is doing with his hands, feet and eyes.

Try not to:

- watch the pupil so intently that you miss important changes in the traffic situation ahead to which your pupil should be responding; or
- watch the road and traffic so intently that you miss faults which are happening in the car.

An effective way of coping with all the visual checks required is to use the MSM, PSL, LAD routines, but from an instructional point of view. For example, when approaching a hazard you should check that your pupil:

M – checks the rear view mirror; look in your own mirror to confirm what is happening behind; check that your pupil acts sensibly on what is seen;

S – is signalling properly, when necessary and at the correct time;

M – manoeuvres;

becomes:

P – positions the vehicle correctly for the situation;

S – slows down to a suitable speed and selects an appropriate gear when necessary;

L – is looking early enough, at the correct time, and that looking is effective and includes using the mirrors;

becomes:

A – assesses the situation correctly;

D – makes a good decision as to how to deal with the hazard.

Continuous assessment should be sensitive to the pupil's needs and is concerned with improving performance. In the last few lessons leading up to the L test, the continuous assessment should give way to 'objective' or 'mock' testing. The purpose of this is to assess the pupil's readiness to take the test and it should be matched to the requirements of the test itself.

GRADING OF ERRORS

Try not to think of errors as being black or white. In driving, there are many shades of grey, and the circumstances surrounding the error need to be taken into account. When assessing driver error, you should take into consideration the following:

- an error can involve varying degrees of importance; and
- some errors are of a more serious nature and can result in more severe consequences than others.

Driver errors will generally fall into one of four categories:

1. **Not marked** – This is where the fault is so slight that you decide not to mention it.
2. **Minor** – This is where the fault does not involve a serious or dangerous situation. No other road-user is involved either potentially or actually.
3. **Serious** – A serious fault is one which involves potential risk to persons or property.
4. **Dangerous** – This is where the actions of the pupil cause actual danger to persons or property.

There is a need for some standardisation between the consistency of assessments made during driving lessons and those used for the driving test. Full details of the Driving Standards Agency fault assessment categories are to be found in *The Driving Instructor's Handbook*.

Having said this, there is no necessity for you to grade errors exactly to DSA test criteria. Remember that we are teaching safe driving for life. Consequently, some instructors may aim for a much higher overall standard of ability than that required on the L test.

This can be beneficial to the pupil. It would be true to say that most learners do not perform as well on the driving test as they do while out with their instructor on lessons. A pupil who has been trained to a higher standard should therefore stand a better chance of passing. Even though he may not drive as well as he can, provided that he does not make any serious or dangerous errors, he may still manage to pass. In any event, the more training a learner has received before taking the test, the better prepared he is likely to be to drive unaccompanied after passing it.

Fault assessment on its own will do little to improve the performance of the learner. To benefit the learner the following procedure should be adopted: 1) Recognise the fault; 2) Analyse the fault; and 3) Correct the fault.

FAULT RECOGNITION

Having recognised the fault, you should identify it as being minor, serious or dangerous. Minor faults can normally be corrected on the move. However, if a recurring pattern of minor faults is identified, you will need to spend some time on dealing with them before they become more serious.

Minor faults could include errors in co-ordination and inefficient or uneconomic driving style, slight inaccuracies in positioning (either travelling along the road or during the set manoeuvres) and harsh use of the controls.

Serious or dangerous faults will need to be discussed more fully. This discussion should be carried out while parked somewhere safe. Do not get into discussions at road junctions, or while the pupil is trying to negotiate hazards – this would only confuse the pupil which could lead to even more serious faults being made.

FAULT ANALYSIS

By the time instructors begin to teach learners, they will have already passed the Part 1 and Part 2 exams. Therefore, their knowledge of what constitutes good driving, and their ability to put it into practice, is already proven.

When analysing faults you therefore need to compare what the pupil is doing, or has done, with what you would be doing or would have done in similar circumstances.

Before analysing the fault you should give some general encouragement to the pupil and feedback on any progress made before the fault occurred. This will make the pupil more receptive to the criticism which you are about to give. Another useful approach, would be to ask the pupil: 'How do you think that drive/manoeuvre went?'.

It may be that the pupil realises that a mistake has been made, in which case you could help the pupil to analyse the fault for himself.

Whichever method you use, you should:

- explain what was wrong (both the cause of the error and its effect and consequences);
- explain what should have happened; and
- explain why it is important (paying particular attention to how the error could affect other road-users etc).

Consider using a visual aid if you need to recreate a difficult situation or explain incorrect positioning on the road, or illustrate how other road-users were involved. Diagrams, models and magnetic boards are useful aids.

After analysing the fault, use your question and answer technique to make sure that the pupil has fully understood what went wrong, what should have happened, and why it is important. This will then lead to the last, and most important, part of the routine.

FAULT CORRECTION

Remedial action will need to be offered while the fault and the improvements needed are still fresh in the pupil's mind. It is of little use to say that you will come back to the fault on the next lesson as by that time the pupil will have probably forgotten what to do.

If the fault involved the way in which the pupil dealt with a particular hazard or junction, the most effective way to correct it would be to get the pupil to approach the same situation again. Depending on the fault, you may decide to talk the pupil through the situation, or just prompt on the points which needed improving. The main thing is that success is achieved. If time allows, a third approach to the same situation, this time leaving the pupil to deal with it entirely unaided, will help to validate your instruction. Praise must be given when improvement has been made.

At the end of each lesson, you should ask yourself:

- Did I identify all the main faults made by my pupil?
- Did I correct all the minor faults on the move and stop to analyse the major faults as soon as convenient?
- Did I analyse the faults made with regard to what went wrong, what should have happened, and why it was important?
- Did I offer appropriate remedial action, bringing about improvement?

4.6

THE USE OF IN-CAR VISUAL/LEARNING AIDS

A learning aid is any medium you might use to enable you to present your ideas, concepts, knowledge and skills in a manner which is more easily understood by your learner.

> *Learning aids can assist the learning process by helping to hold the learner's attention and generate an interest which stimulates the desire to learn.*

It has been said that, 'The purpose of a learning aid is to liberate the teacher from the limitations of his own speech'. But, while learning aids may help to make a good instructor even better, they will not compensate for bad teaching.

Learning aids range from a simple notepad and pencil to sophisticated driving simulators. Between these two extremes, there is a vast range of aids available to the instructor, many of which are visual. In this section we will concentrate on those aids of a visual nature which can be used in the car.

'A picture paints a thousand words' - provided it is a good picture! It is amazing how many instructors say to their pupils: 'I am not very good at drawing, but I am going to draw you a diagram to explain what I mean'.

Visual aids for the classroom are covered later in this chapter. Most of the traditional classroom visual aids to learning have been adapted for use in the car. These include:

- dry-wipe boards and markers;
- pre-prepared diagrams;
- photographs or diagrams in books;
- magnetic boards and models;
- a 'steerable' model car (this is particularly useful for explaining the principles of steering in reverse);
- model clutches; and
- steering aids ('static steer' or a simple round tea-tray) which can be used for demonstration and practice .

The visual aids you use are limited only by your imagination. You can use your hands to explain how the clutch plates come together; you can use your fingers to show 'the thickness of a coin' when explaining the biting point; you can produce pre-prepared diagrams to assist you in explaining various aspects of road procedure, manoeuvres etc.

Be careful, however, not to over-use visual aids to the extent that they detract from the basic message you wish to put across.

Visual aids offer the following benefits:

- they add structure to your lesson;
- they provide a change of activity for the learner;
- they will assist you by reminding you what needs to be said;
- they will allow the pupil to recall and visualise previously encountered situations;
- they can help to clarify difficult concepts or show specific positions required when manoeuvring or dealing with hazards; and
- they stimulate the interest of the learner and help to maintain attention.

> *By being skilful in designing, creating and integrating visual aids in your presentation, you will be able to bring the lesson to life.*

When using visual aids in the car you should:

- avoid just reading from a script;
- talk to the pupil and not to the visual aid;
- turn the aid around so that the pupil can see it – it is for their benefit, not just for yours;
- avoid covering the visual aid with your hand – you may need to hold it with your right hand and use your left hand, or a pen, to point to the key parts;
- avoid 'pen-waving' because it can be threatening to the pupil; and
- once you have used the aid, put it away before it becomes a distraction.

The following ABC of visual aids use should be borne in mind:

ACCURACY – Try to ensure that the visual aid accurately recreates the situation you are trying to depict.

BREVITY – Keep drawings/diagrams simple and avoid having too many words or unnecessary detail.

CLARITY – Ensure that letters or words are big enough to be seen by the pupil without the need for reading glasses.

DELETION – Use them then lose them, otherwise they become a distraction.

EMPHASIS – Make sure that the visual aid stresses the key points.

At the end of each lesson ask yourself:

- Did I take every opportunity to use visual aids in order to assist the learning process?
- Were the visual aids used, stimulating and effective?
- Did I identify any situations where a visual aid could have been useful? If so, should I think about designing one for future use?

4.7

EXPLANATION, DEMONSTRATION, PRACTICE ROUTINE

When teaching a skill as complicated as driving a car, you must have clearly in mind all the component parts of the skill. Before attempting to teach the skill, you will need to ask:

1. What knowledge does the learner need in order to carry out the task successfully?
2. What attitudes should the learner have towards carrying out the task?
3. What manipulative and/or perceptive skills does the task involve?

Each component part of the skill will have a 'prepared' position from which the actual performance commences. This may involve positioning of the hands and/or feet and the use of the eyes in anticipation of carrying out the specific task. Being poised ready for action can be important from the point of view of smoothness, control, accuracy and safety.

For example, moving off requires the car to be in a 'prepared state': ie, gear selected, gas set, clutch to biting point, handbrake prepared. This will be followed by checking ahead, checking mirrors, checking blindspots, assessing whether it is safe to go and whether a signal is necessary, releasing the handbrake, slowly bringing the clutch up and increasing the gas, and putting the hand back onto the steering wheel.

To help the learner to memorise this sequence, the following mnemonic could be used:

$$P \text{ (Prepare)} - O \text{ (Observe)} - M \text{ (Move)}$$

An experienced driver gets into the car, starts up and moves off in a matter of seconds without having to think what he is doing.

For the novice, things are not so simple. As the moving off procedure and the co-ordination of the clutch and gas is so vital for many of the other driving tasks to follow, much practice will be needed to get it right.

With all these basic formative skills most pupils will benefit from a demonstration. It is all too easy for the instructor to assume that the pupil knows, understands, and can do what is required. The many wives who have ended up in tears after being taught how to move off by their husbands bear witness to this. Invariably they end up knocking on your door for help.

Prior to practising a new skill the learner should understand WHY it has to be learnt; WHEN and WHERE it should be applied; he should clearly understand WHAT is expected of him and HOW the skill is to be performed.

The most effective sequence of skill training is: 1) EXPLANATION, 2) DEMONSTRATION, and 3) PRACTICE. This teaching routine is a prime example of how many of the PTS in this book can be brought together to form a strategy for learning.

EXPLANATION

Briefings and explanations have been covered more fully in chapter 3. The explanation should be tailored to take account of the level of ability of the learner. During the early stages of learning to drive, it might sometimes be better to concentrate on the KEY POINTS, so that the pupil is not OVERLOADED with information.

Once these key points are fully established it will be easier for the learner to understand and retain additional information given at a later date.

Most explanations will need to include the following: CONTROL *(of the vehicle);* OBSERVATIONS *(hazard recognition, other road-users and attitudes towards them); and* ACCURACY *(positioning and steering of the vehicle).*

CONTROL – Briefings will need to cover control of the vehicle and speed approaching or dealing with hazards. This should include the manipulative aspects of driving; co-ordination of controls; smoothness; securing the vehicle when stationary.

OBSERVATIONS – This will contain necessary information on the LOOK, ASSESS, DECIDE routine; skills of perception; safety margins; attitudes towards other road-users.

ACCURACY – This section will cover aspects of steering; positioning and general accuracy; course and lane discipline where appropriate.

Visual aids

Although we have dealt with visual aids in the previous section, they should be mentioned again here. Any aids or diagrams which will clarify, reinforce, or give authority to an explanation should be used. You may find it useful to refer to the main published authorities on driving:

> *The Highway Code*
> *Your Driving Test*
> *The Driving Manual*

These can be used to 'add weight to your words'.

DEMONSTRATION

A demonstration is useful in that the learner will be able to see a model of correct behaviour which he can then imitate. Complex tasks can be broken down into component parts which can be demonstrated before the learner practises and repeats them until mastery is achieved. The advantages of you giving a demonstration are:

- you can adapt the demonstration to suit the specific needs of the pupil; and
- you are there to answer any questions which the pupil may wish to ask.

The demonstration must not be used to dazzle the learner with your own expertise. The key points in the preceding briefing or explanation should form an integral part of the demonstration by way of an abbreviated commentary.

A learner may often be genuinely unaware of a mistake. A demonstration will help to show learners where they are going wrong and what is needed to correct the problem. This is especially so when the pupil's perception of safety margins; the need for 'holding back' procedures; and speed approaching hazards, is poor.

You might mention slowing down approaching a hazard and get no response from the learner if your pupil's understanding of 'slow' is different from your own. Under these circumstances a demonstration can be a valuable aid to you in persuading the pupil to modify what he is doing to fit in with what you want him to do.

It may be helpful to your pupil if you SIMULATE what he is doing wrong. You can then demonstrate what he *should* be doing so that he can see the difference.

This technique would be particularly useful when giving feedback on the pupil's performance in the set manoeuvres.

Points to remember

1. Explain beforehand why you are going to demonstrate and what it is all about.
2. Pitch the demonstration and the commentary given while carrying it out to the correct level for the ability of the learner.
3. Make the demonstration as perfect an example as possible of what you want the pupil to do.
4. Restrict the commentary to key points only and those that are necessary for that particular learner.
5. Consolidate afterwards with a debriefing and controlled practice.

The demonstration should be concluded with a summary of the key points which might then lead to a Q/A session to identify any aspects of the task which the learner still does not understand.

PRACTICE

Having demonstrated the skill you should then allow your pupil to practice it as soon as possible. The first time the pupil attempts the skill, it is important that success is achieved.

There is nothing more demotivating for a learner than to watch you carry out a task perfectly and then to fail miserably trying to copy it. You will therefore need to prompt the pupil as soon as you see that they are encountering difficulties or deviating from what they should be doing. For example, if the pupil is practising the turn in the road and not turning the wheel effectively, you may need to say: 'Use longer movements of the steering wheel and turn more briskly'.

> *Establishing good habits in these early stages while practising the manoeuvre will pay dividends for the learner later on.*

When the pupil is practising new skills, carefully watch their body language for signs of stress, frustration or despair. Be prepared to intervene if necessary. Encouragement and reassurance may be needed. Be prepared to change tack and go back to consolidating previously learnt skills to boost flagging confidence.

Controlled practice will allow the beginner to remain safe, and not be too unsympathetic to the vehicle. It involves the learner in following simple verbal instructions to carry out the component parts of the skill which, when brought together, form complete mastery.

The speed with which the learner interprets and responds to the instruction needs to be taken into account. This may vary from pupil to pupil. With some pupils it may be necessary to carry out tasks more slowly than normal.

The instructions given should eventually be reduced to prompting. As soon as the learner appears to be able to cope for himself, the instruction should gradually be phased out.

The amount of prompting given will depend on the ability and willingness of the learner to make decisions for himself. Some learners will require a lot of encouragement to act and think for themselves.

> *The ultimate objective is to get the learner to carry out each skill under all normal traffic conditions with no prompting from you at all.*

Many learners approach the driving test being able to do all the things required of them, but doing them all badly. This does not help the learners who may themselves be aware that things are 'not quite right'. If you cannot or will not help them to improve, do not be surprised if having failed the test, they decide to go somewhere else for lessons!

The sequence of development should be:

> CONTROLLED PRACTICE;
> PROMPTED PRACTICE;
> TRANSFERRED RESPONSIBILITY;
> REFLECTION; then
> REVISION.

Prompting should not be necessary where the learner is about to be presented for the L test!

After using the EDP routine, you will need to ask yourself:

- Did I use the EDP routine to good effect?
- Did my briefing or explanations cover all the key points?
- Did my demonstration have the desired effect on the pupil?
- Did I assist my pupil to achieve initial success by prompting when necessary?
- Did I take account of the body language of the pupil when practising new skills?
- Am I flexible enough to change back to previously learnt skills in order to boost confidence?
- Did I transfer responsibility as soon as it was appropriate to do so, or did I 'keep instructing' when it was no longer necessary?

4.8

SELLING IDEAS AND CONCEPTS

In driving instruction, selling skills go far beyond being able to persuade potential pupils to book driving lessons with your school.

Development of your Practical Teaching Skills will enable you to become more effective when selling ideas and concepts to your pupils when you are teaching in the car on a one-to-one basis. In this book we are going to concentrate on this aspect of selling.

Everybody has sold something at some time in their lives, and everybody is involved with selling whether they realise it or not.

Selling in the car is much more informal than selling generally. Although simple instinct will help you when selling ideas, the development and controlled use of many of the communication skills will improve your ability to convince others that they should 'buy' your ideas and concepts, as well as your driving lessons.

> *Remember the good instructor must be able to persuade his pupils to do what it is that he wants them to do, in the way that he wants them to do it!*

When selling informally on a one-to-one basis, if you are skilful, you will involve the pupil in what is happening by explaining to him the benefits of following your advice and doing things your way, and listening to his response.

When selling ideas or concepts, you must be as knowledgeable as possible about the issue under discussion and will need to make good use of your communication skills, especially:

- your verbal communication skills;
- your listening skills; and
- your use of positive body language and the interpretation of the body language of your pupils.

When selling ideas you first of all need to explain WHAT it is that you require your pupil to do or understand; second comes HOW you want whatever is being done to be carried out and, third, WHY it is important that it is carried out in a particular way.

The most important of these is WHY. There is no point in the pupil knowing what he is supposed to be doing if he doesn't know why he should do it in a certain way.

The skilful, and two-way, use of the question and answer technique will help you to achieve all three objectives.

> *The good instructor will help the pupil to arrive at conclusions for himself by guiding the discussion.*

As in selling services, any objections should be dealt with by further questioning and explanation so it is very important that you listen carefully to everything the pupil says. You must try to draw the pupil into the discussion rather than lecture him.

When sat at the side of the road or in the classroom, the body language you use when selling ideas must be positive and support and endorse what you are saying. For example:

- forceful hand gestures may be used to emphasise important points;
- strong eye contact should be made to show your sincerity and belief in what you are saying: and
- nods of approval coupled with smiles should be given when the pupil reaches good conclusions – this will encourage the pupil to participate further.

You should watch carefully the body language of the pupil to help you identify any resistance to your ideas or concepts.

If such resistance is detected, question the pupil: 'You don't seem very happy with that. What's the problem?'

Once you have identified the problem, you should handle it like any other objection, outlining the benefits of doing things or seeing things your way. Don't forget the benefits will nearly always relate to SAFETY, CONVENIENCE and COST SAVINGS.

For example, you might be trying to convince a pupil that he really doesn't have to signal every time he moves off when there is no other road-user in sight.

The debriefing might go something like this:

'OK Julie, how do you think that drive went?'

'Well, I don't think it was too bad. I know I was a bit jerky with the clutch when I moved off.'

'Yes, it was a little bit jerky but we can always work on that and it will get better with practice. I liked the way you waited for the red car coming from behind to pass before you moved off, but do you really think you needed to signal?

'Well my dad said it's always best to signal just in case.'

'Yes I agree that if it had been a busy High Street a signal might have been a good idea, but you did check your blind spot again and nothing was coming. I had a pupil on test the other week and the examiner stopped her on a busy road to give his next instructions. Before moving off again, the pupil checked her mirror, saw a bus coming along so decided to give a signal for moving off. The bus driver realised the learner might have been on test and decided to stop for her. The pupil then got confused and didn't know whether to go or wait. In the meantime the bus driver got fed up with waiting and started to move off again. At the same time, the pupil decided to move off and the examiner had to intervene. If the pupil had assessed the situation correctly and not signalled there wouldn't have been a problem would there? If there was a bus coming you wouldn't move off in any case would you?'

'No, not really!'

'Good. Well let's try moving off again. This time I'd like you to assess the situation yourself, and then decide if you need to signal. If you are not sure, then it would be best to signal but get used to assessing situations and making decisions based on safety. Does that make sense?'

At the end of each lesson where you have had to sell ideas or concepts to your pupils, analyse your own performance by asking yourself:

- Have I used my selling skills to good effect, and successfully convinced my pupil WHY it is important that they see or do things my way?

4.9

VERBAL AND PHYSICAL INTERVENTION

Some learner drivers may fail to recognise potentially dangerous traffic situations in time to employ the necessary procedure or defensive strategy.

> *Not only should instructors read the road well ahead, but they must also learn to anticipate an incorrect response by the learner to the situation and be prepared to compensate for it, either by verbal or physical action.*

When giving driving lessons you must maintain a safe learning environment for your pupils by:

- planning routes commensurate with their ability;
- forward planning and concentrating on the overall traffic situation – front, rear and to the sides;
- being alert and anticipating learners' incorrect actions or lack of activity in difficult situations;
- giving clear directions in good time for them to respond;
- overriding learners' decisions when necessary; and
- being prepared to intervene verbally or physically.

Many learners show a reluctance to slow down, give way, stop, or hold back when necessary. This is usually because they have an innate fear of stopping. If they stop, they know they have then got to get the car moving again – one of the most difficult things for learners to do in the early stages!

This reluctance to deal with hazards defensively may cause the situation to develop into an emergency. Where the situation is allowed to reach this critical level, there are two possible unwanted reactions from the learner: 1) He may do nothing and remain frozen at the controls on a collision course or 2) He may over-react at the last minute and this could result in harsh, uncontrolled braking, the effect of which is difficult to predict.

It is in situations like this that the professional instructor proves his or her worth. By intervening, either verbally or physically, a possible accident situation can be avoided.

There are four main reasons why you should intervene:

1. To prevent risk of injury or damage to persons or property (including the driving school car).
2. To prevent the pupil from breaking the law which could lead to you being prosecuted for 'aiding and abetting'.
3. To prevent excessive stress to the learner in certain unplanned circumstances (for example, an emergency situation).
4. To prevent mechanical damage to the vehicle (for example, in the event of an injudicious gear change).

Because intervention can undermine confidence and inhibit the progress of the learner, it should be kept to a minimum. Verbal intervention should, if time allows, be used before considering the use of physical intervention or the dual controls.

VERBAL INTERVENTION

A verbal instruction or command will usually be successful in dealing with most traffic situations or driver errors, providing it is given early enough.

Verbal instructions and memory prompts will be used more frequently in the early stages of learning to drive, and may take the form of more specific instructions such as: 'Use the mirrors *well* before . . .', 'More brake!', 'Ease off the brake' and 'Clutch down'.

These more positive commands will often be needed to make sure that your pupil slows down early enough on the approach to a potential hazard.

'Hold back!', 'Give way!' and 'Wait!' are other examples of *positive* instructions which require a *positive* response or reaction from the pupil, but which also leave him some freedom of judgement.

When using this type of command, the pitch and tone of your voice should be used to convey the degree of urgency to the pupil.

The use of the word 'Stop' should generally be restricted to those occasions when other instructions have not been followed by the pupil or when the pupil has not responded positively. Incorrect use of this command could mean that your pupil over-reacts and stops too suddenly or in an unsuitable position. Unnecessary and too frequent use of the word 'Stop' – for example, when parking – could have the effect that pupils will not respond quickly enough in urgent situations.

PHYSICAL INTERVENTION

Use of any form of physical intervention or the dual controls should be restricted to situations when the verbal instruction has not been followed or there is insufficient time for it to be given by the instructor or acted on by the pupil.

In these situations, you may need to consider the main alternatives:

- use of the dual brake and/or clutch; or
- assistance with the steering.

Using the dual brake/clutch
The following points need to be considered:

- Avoid sitting with your legs crossed when teaching. When approaching hazards, keep your right foot discreetly near the dual brake but not riding on it.
- Avoid unnecessary or 'fidgety' movements of your feet as this may unnerve your pupil.
- Only use the dual clutch when it is absolutely necessary and *never* to 'make things easy' for the pupil.
- Make effective use of the dual mirror before using the dual brake.
- If your pupil has 'frozen' on the gas pedal, avoid using the dual clutch as this could cause a blown head gasket.
- Give the pupil time to use the brake before intervening. If you both use the brake at the same time, this could cause problems.
- Consider using the dual brake to help you to 'buy time' if you have to help with the steering. This applies particularly where the pupil may be trying to turn a corner too fast.

Assistance with steering
This should only be used to make slight alterations to road position. It would be better for you to tell the pupil to 'Steer to the right' or 'Steer to the left'.

Bear in mind the following points:

- Minor corrections with steering are usually more practical and safer alternatives to using the dual brake.
- Use only your right hand when assisting with steering.
- Avoid physical contact. If you get hold of the pupil's hand or arm and they let go of the wheel, you have lost control.
- If you wish to steer to the left, hold the wheel near the top so that you can 'pull down'.
- If you wish to steer to the right, hold the wheel near the bottom so that you can 'push up'.
- If the situation is such that more drastic turning of the wheel is required, it would be safer and much less worrying for the pupil if you used the dual brake.
- Never get into a fight with the pupil over the wheel – you might lose!

There may be occasions when assistance with both steering and braking are required. For example, it may be essential to hold the steering wheel while using the dual brake to prevent the pupil from oversteering. In order to gain more time, you may need to reduce and control the speed of the vehicle with the dual brake, particularly when the pupil has 'frozen' on the gas pedal.

In any potentially dangerous situation, you will need to use your experience to decide which method of intervention is required. You may need to use the dual clutch at the same time as manipulating the gear lever to prevent an inappropriate gear change. This will allow your pupil to concentrate on maintaining the correct speed and position.

Examples of other types of physical intervention which do crop up from time to time are:

- selecting a missed gear at a critical time or place;
- preventing an incorrect gear selection by 'covering the gear lever' until the correct speed is reached;
- covering the dual clutch so as to be ready to prevent the car moving off at an inappropriate time;
- rectifying an error with the handbrake when there is no time to tell the pupil to do so;
- switching off the engine to prevent mechanical damage;
- cancelling an injudicious signal with safety in mind and there is no time to tell the pupil to do so.

The need for any kind of intervention can be kept to an absolute minimum by careful route planning and matching the road and traffic conditions to the ability of the pupil.

You may encounter some resentment against any form of physical interference or the use of the dual controls. This could result in the pupil losing confidence in themselves and in you as a teacher. You should therefore make sure that:

- you do not get into the habit of using physical intervention or the dual controls excessively or unnecessarily;
- having used any physical intervention, you fully explain to the pupil WHAT you did to control the car, and WHY it was necessary to do it!

4.10

DEVISING TESTS

All teachers require some skill and understanding in using techniques for assessing learning achievement and its outcomes. Driving instructors are no exception. This is particularly so in the UK where the driver training system that has evolved tends to start with the L test, and then look at what training should take place in order for the learner to be able to pass that test.

> *In an ideal world, learning to drive should start with the training programme, which should culminate in the learner taking a test which validates that training.*

Tests usually form important elements of assessment procedures, but testing and assessing are not the same thing. Tests are often used for employment reasons – measuring suitability etc. They can also be used for learning purposes. In this book, we will concentrate on devising tests for learning purposes.

Using tests is a complex subject. (The theory of testing is covered in *The Driving Instructor's Handbook*.) It is possible to assess every aspect of learning. The purpose of tests is to 'sample' what learning has taken place.

Many instructors will find themselves preparing students for tests and examinations set by external bodies, such as the DSA, IAM, RoSPA, AEB, City & Guilds etc. Some examinations will encourage rote learning of the questions and answers required to pass, and 'knowing what the examiners are looking for'. Trainers, instructors, ADIs and learners may try to out-guess the examiner in what becomes an elaborate game.

When tests are devised and administered internally, teachers or trainers know what is to be sampled, select accordingly, and prepare their students for those tests. In this way, assessment drives the learning.

Testing is rather like taking snap-shots of progress at moments in time along the learning journey. For example, an instructor taking a Check Test could get a grade five with a novice pupil, teaching one particular subject, at a particular time of the day, in a particular place, in one set of weather, road and traffic conditions, and with one particular examiner. If the same instructor were Check Tested while giving a different lesson – to a pupil with different ability, on a different day and time, in a different place with different road, traffic and weather conditions, and with a different examiner – it is possible that he could get a different grading.

The purpose of this section is to indicate to you how to devise tests that will be useful in bringing about learning.

Modern thinking in assessment and testing is that learners or trainees should be measured on how competent they are against the objectives set. The whole NVQ revolution has gone away from assessing what people know, moving towards what people can do. Units of competence are designed by the trainer to assist in this process.

> *For driving instruction purposes, tests should be designed to show what a learner can do or how a learner is doing. They need to be* VALID *and* RELIABLE.

Test validity

This should be linked to course objectives, measuring the competence of the learner against the objectives set. Test validity can be defined as the degree to which a test measures what it is intended to measure. For example, if you asked a learner to write out the complete procedure for reversing into a limited opening on the left, he may do a very good job. He might detail the control required; cover all the observations necessary; and the degree of accuracy needed. However, this would not be a valid test of his ability to carry out the manoeuvre. It would merely prove that he knew the theory of how to do it.

Test reliability

This can be defined as the degree to which a test *consistently* measures what it is intended to measure. General factors which may affect reliability include the objectivity of the test and the environment in which the test is taking place.

Other factors which cause tests to be unreliable include those which are:

Instructor related – ambiguity of directions and instructions given; poor timing of instructions or directions given; or

Pupil related – physical state; emotional condition; exam nerves.

Apart from continuous assessment of pupils by the instructor during driving lessons, the following tests will be useful:

- initial assessments;
- question and answer tests;
- *Highway Code* and driving related tests;
- practical assessments; and
- mock driving tests.

When devising any of the above tests, bear in mind the validity and reliability of the end product.

The 'Halo' effect

When teaching learners on a one-to-one basis, it is impossible to remove the human element from driver assessments. If you develop a particular regard for a pupil with whom you get on well, it is possible to subconsciously ignore minor errors, or even those of a more serious nature. If this happens, you have lost your objectivity. You may even find yourself choosing an easier route for the favoured pupil, avoiding difficult traffic situations.

Usually, accepting that the 'halo effect' exists will lessen the likelihood of it happening. If you do not remain objective, the pupil will suffer in the long run.

The opposite can occur with an unpopular client. In this case you may find yourself treating relatively minor errors as more serious ones and perhaps fail to acknowledge improvements, and not give praise where it is due.

Assessment records

At any one time you could have about 30 or 40 pupils, or even more if you are running a school. Each one is likely to be at a different stage of learning and even those at similar stages may not have covered identical aspects of driving in exactly the same order. In addition, your students will have a wide range of abilities and aptitude and will all have their own personal likes and dislikes.

For teaching purposes alone, information on assessment and testing will help you to create suitable and effective learning experiences for each pupil. This is particularly important when carrying out more formal training such as intensive courses or instructor training.

Record keeping for instructors is covered in chapter 9 of this book and in *The Driving Instructor's Handbook*.

4.11

SETTING TASKS FOR IN BETWEEN LESSONS

A large number of new drivers still leave learning the *Highway Code* rules until just prior to taking their test. This only encourages people to learn to recite them 'parrot fashion' to the driving examiner without really understanding their meaning.

Teaching people how to drive, as you will now be well aware, is not just a matter of developing their practical skills. In order to be able to drive safely, your pupils must become aware of the importance of understanding, and being able to apply safely, the rules of the road.

Motivation is an extremely important factor in learning to drive. You should stress that the better the pupil understands the meaning of the rules, then the quicker they will learn how to apply them. It may also be beneficial to point out that if they do not study in between their lessons, you will need to take time out from their driving practice to go over the rules in the car. This will probably result in them needing more lessons, meaning greater costs.

Where pupils are reluctant to get involved with studying, you will need to sell the 'Safe Driving for Life' message. To encourage understanding you should set between-lesson tasks which involve studying *Your Driving Test*, *The Driving Manual* and the *Highway Code*.

> *The tasks set should involve reading the rules and routines which relate directly to what the pupil is currently learning to put into practice during their on-road lessons.*

This will allow them to 'link in' the theory to the practice.

For example, prior to a lesson dealing with emerging at road junctions, ask the pupil to learn the rules relating to the markings at the end of roads. This should help them identify and understand the meaning of these as they approach the different types of junctions.

Learn to Drive in 10 Easy Stages by Margaret Stacey, published by Kogan Page, London, 1993, is a simple guide which helps with between-lesson study and practice by stating the key points for each subject and listing the relevant *Highway Code* rules and sections of *Your Driving Test*. By providing 'tick boxes' it involves the pupil and instructor in assessing the pupil's progress at each stage.

At the end of each lesson give the pupil a unit of study, which should be in written format so that it is not forgotten. Refer them to the particular rules or sections of each book to be studied. To validate whether learning has taken place, you can either include a short question paper with each task set or ask a few questions at the beginning of the next lesson.

Set some questions which do not have simple answers so that discussion can take place in order to encourage the development of safe attitudes. Avoid questions which the pupil may think are set to trick as this will only demotivate the pupil. An example of the type of question you could ask to encourage and stimulate their thinking processes would be: 'What are the speed limits for and why should we obey them?'.

Where questions are answered incorrectly you should explain the reasoning behind the correct answer – remember you are teaching the pupil how to 'understand'.

Tasks set should be easily attainable for each individual pupil. Remember, learning should be a two-way effort with both of you working together to attain the same goal. If you have pupils with learning problems, encourage someone in the family to help with their between-lesson studies. Try not to overload them with too much theoretical work so that learning to drive becomes no longer enjoyable.

Approaching the test, you may need to 'step up' the between-lesson tasks if the pupil's level of knowledge is still weak.

Where pupils are gaining extra between-lesson practice, their supervising drivers should also be made aware of their current needs. It could be useful to invite them to sit in on a lesson to observe what you are teaching the pupil, and how and why you are teaching it.

This would be particularly useful where advice given by the supervisor has been at variance with what you have been teaching. By getting the experienced driver to watch you, any further practice the pupil may receive can be linked in to consolidate the new skills.

If pupils have any particular weaknesses, you can outline those subjects which they need to practice. This could prove beneficial to the supervising driver who may learn about methods and procedures which have changed since they passed their test. It may also make them aware of the need to keep up to date with defensive driving techniques and the changing rules and regulations.

This is likely to have a spin-off road safety benefit through 'updating' the supervising driver and making him more aware of current attitudes towards driving!

4.12

TEACHING BASIC CAR MECHANICS AND MAINTENANCE

One of the topics included in the DSA's syllabus for learning to drive is 'Car controls, equipment and components'. Although, as a driving instructor, you do not need to know how every component in your car works, or how to carry out repairs, you should be able to teach your pupils some of the more basic principles and procedures.

Teaching a basic knowledge of how the car works will help your pupils develop vehicle sympathy. Showing them how to carry out routine checks and identify defects should also avoid unnecessary delays and breakdowns for them.

The Driving Instructor's Handbook contains a complete chapter on the car and you can use this as a reference source, along with your own vehicle handbook, when you are preparing your lesson plans.

Items which you could cover include:

- re-fuelling the car;
- checking oil, water and fluid levels;
- checking tyre pressures and condition;
- checking bulbs and replacing them;
- wheel changing;
- routine preventative maintenance.

If you have the appropriate level of knowledge and skills, you might even consider taking things a little further and teach the more enthusiastic new drivers basic maintenance and servicing requirements.

The way in which you teach this subject will depend entirely on whether you wish to cover it on an individual basis, or whether you wish to teach it to groups of pupils.

On a 'one-to-one' basis you can combine an educational re-fuelling stop with showing your pupils how to make the basic checks and bulb replacements. If you intend to go a little deeper into the subject and teach it in groups, you will need to either use your own garage or locate suitable premises where you will have the space to work in.

For more comprehensive coverage of car mechanics you might even consider hiring classroom facilities and obtaining models of different parts of the car to show how they work.

By helping your pupils to develop a sympathetic attitude towards the car they are more likely to drive economically and safely.

4.13

TEACHING IN THE CLASSROOM

Many driving instructors view teaching in the classroom as being pure theory training, and teaching in the car as practical instruction. This is largely due to the haphazard way in which driving instruction in this country has evolved over the years.

When teaching takes place in the car or in the classroom, there are both theoretical and practical components which should be covered by the teacher.

Some instructors already teach in adult education centres, instructor training centres or in secondary schools, giving pre-driver training. With the introduction of a separate theory test for learner drivers, teaching in the classroom should become a requirement for more driving instructors.

Solo driving instructors may have to band together to provide classroom facilities. The PTS in this book will be invaluable when teaching in the classroom.

The teacher is responsible for managing the environment, the available resources and the instruction given, so that pupils may learn as effectively as possible.

In-class sessions should be made as practical as possible and linked to in-car practice. The following aspects will need to be borne in mind.

Teacher Activity

As the classroom teacher, you will need to:

- prepare the lesson plan;
- be punctual (allow time to check equipment);
- dress appropriately;
- ensure that any new students know your name;
- keep a register if the lesson is one of a series of lessons so that attendance and progress can be monitored; and
- deliver the lesson.

The classroom

You must give consideration to:

- size, lighting, heating, ventilation, provision of drinking water;
- seating arrangement (be prepared to rearrange the seating layout from time to time to avoid social cliques forming and to suit the activity you have planned);
- equipment needed for the lesson – power points, extension leads, window blinds etc; and
- health and safety requirements – fire extinguisher, fire certificate and details of fire drill, toilet/washing facilities, safety of electrical equipment and leads

Teaching/visual aids

These will need to be checked before the lesson if they are to be used and may include:

- black-/whiteboards, flip charts, chalk, markers etc;
- overhead projectors and transparencies;
- slide projectors and slides;
- film projectors and films;
- charts, diagrams, magnetic boards, models etc; and
- pre-prepared hand-outs.

The following rules will assist you in using any of the above teaching/visual aids effectively:

ACCURACY – Keep them factual and accurate.
BREVITY – Keep them simple, avoiding unnecessary detail.

CLARITY – Ensure that any lettering is big enough to be seen clearly.

DELETION – Use them, then lose them – otherwise they become a distraction.

EMPHASIS – Stress the key points.

FEEDBACK – Carefully watch the student's reaction to the visual aids used so that you can evaluate their impact and effectiveness.

Teaching methods

You must avoid DOMINATING the lesson. Although teacher-centred learning can be useful in the early stages of learning or at the beginning of a given lesson, it will not assist the full development of the capabilities of your students.

Your learners will come to the classroom with needs and expectations which they hope to fulfil. These include:

- social needs, such as working in groups and competing with others;
- the desire to make progress and improve themselves; and
- the need to satisfy curiosity and perform tasks well.

The good teacher will make the learning PUPIL CENTRED by involving the students as much as possible and catering for the individual needs of each student where possible. This will be best achieved by you 'guiding' your students to reach their own conclusions, thus developing their abilities, building on strengths and improving any weaknesses.

Preparing the lesson plan

When preparing a classroom lesson you should consider:

- an introduction;
- the development of the subject;
- a conclusion; and
- setting any homework.

An introduction

You should aim to get your class members working together as soon as possible. This will lessen the likelihood of social chatter, thus putting the amount of time available to best use.

The introduction should therefore be as short as possible, perhaps recapping on what was covered in the previous lesson by using the

Q/A technique. The basic principles covering the aims and objectives of the lesson being given could then be outlined.

The development of the subject

This should actively involve the students in learning from the known to the unknown; building up knowledge progressively; moving from the simple to the more difficult.

Pupil activity could include: note taking; discussions; practising; Q/A sessions; stimulating games; role-play exercises; and a quiz or test.

You could deal with any homework set the previous week during the lesson, involving all members of the class, rather than marking it individually. However, if this method is used, you should invite those members of the class who have done written or project work to leave it for marking and return it to them at the start of the next lesson.

A conclusion

When concluding the lesson, you should consolidate any new information, knowledge or attitudes taught either by random Q/A sessions or by using a prepared list of questions.

This will allow you to evaluate your teaching, and how much learning has taken place. It should also reinforce the key points, stimulate the brighter students, and encourage the less able students to demonstrate what they have learnt.

Setting homework

Any homework set should be designed to consolidate the subject matter of the lesson given. Try to avoid making homework purely academic. Project work can be set to be dealt with during the next lesson, or homework could include some practical application of what has been taught.

Delivering the lesson

By using the PTS outlined in this book, you should be able to deliver a lesson to a class of students in an efficient and effective way.

Even if you are used to teaching groups, you will often feel nervous at the start of a lesson. This is perfectly normal but, as the lesson develops, your natural enthusiasm should take over and things should become more relaxed.

Provided the lesson has been prepared properly, and your notes are to hand, things should run reasonably smoothly.

A glass of water should be kept handy so that if you do 'dry up' you can take a quick drink and gather your thoughts. A packet of mints can also come in useful.

Try to make eye contact with each student in turn and speak to the class as if you are speaking to individuals. Don't be panicked by periods of silence – these can be useful and add impact and importance to what you are saying.

When using the blackboard or whiteboard, try not to cover up what you are writing or showing the class. Avoid talking to the class as you are writing on the board.

If you have a 'rollerboard' available it is sometimes useful to write your material on it before the lesson, as long as you do not roll it down and display it before you need it or forget to lose it after you've used it.

When asking questions use the POSE – PAUSE – POUNCE technique.

POSE the question to the class generally;
PAUSE for them to think about it; and
POUNCE on the member of the class you wish to answer it.

Make sure that you spread your questions evenly around the group, giving everybody a chance to participate, especially the quieter members of the class.

After the lesson has finished analyse your own performance. If you can video the proceedings this will be very useful in evaluating how well you have delivered the lesson. Ask yourself:

- How well did I present myself to the class?
- Was the classroom laid out in an efficient way?
- Were the teaching/visual aids suitable for the lesson being given, and were they used effectively?
- Were the teaching methods used suitable for the group?
- How well did I prepare the lesson plan?
- Was the lesson delivered efficiently and effectively?

4.14

GROUP WORK SKILLS

Driving instructors often choose not to work in groups, preferring to teach on a one-to-one basis.

There may be, however, times in your life when you will have to work in a group, whether it be a group of local instructors, a local or national association, a group committee, or perhaps the parent/teachers' association of your children's school. In these situations you will be responsible for completing certain tasks which contribute to the effectiveness of the group as a whole.

The interactive skills which will be required in these situations are highly transferable and will be useful on many other occasions in both your business and personal life.

To work effectively within a group, the interactive PTS in this book will help you to:

- present yourself well to others;
- adopt an open attitude;
- be sensitive to the feelings and needs of others;
- allow an equal opportunity for all to contribute;
- accept criticisms;
- work with self-confidence; and
- acknowledge the role of the group leader.

In this section we will be dealing with: The nature of groups; Leading a group; and Developing groups.

THE NATURE OF GROUPS

Forming groups goes back to our cave-dwelling days and is a natural process for most human beings. Most individuals seek the companionship and friendship of other people for a variety of reasons, both at work and in leisure.

Irrespective of whether a group is FORMAL or INFORMAL, OPEN or CLOSED, being a member of a group offers numerous advantages.

- Groups often accomplish tasks more effectively than individuals by allowing people to pool their resources and experience.
- By relying on the expertise of fellow members, individuals feel more secure when making decisions and taking action within the group.
- Groups provide emotional support which is not always available when working as an individual.
- Groups provide a sense of identity, thus increasing self-esteem and self-confidence and giving credibility to the individual.

Members often choose to wear badges, ties etc to display their allegiance to the group.
- A great sense of pride can come from being a member of a group, particularly where there are entry qualifications and requirements.

LEADING A GROUP

Some groups require one member to act as leader. The leader is usually responsible for ensuring that the groups' activities assist in achieving its aims and objectives.

If the members of a group challenge its leadership, the group cannot function effectively. The group leader must therefore establish effective working relationships with most of the members of the group.

To successfully lead a group a number of responsibilities have to be accepted:

- Setting group aims and objectives.
- Agreeing mutually acceptable responsibilities for individual group members.
- Negotiating responsibilities with members.
- Consulting with group members on their progress in reaching individual targets.
- Motivating the group.
- Encouraging communication and co-operation within and outside the group.
- Solving problems and making decisions.
- Accepting the views, opinions and ideas of the group.
- Encouraging initiative within the group.
- Creating a harmonious working environment.
- Disciplining group members when necessary.

It is questionable whether good leaders are born or whether they can be trained. There is no doubt that by developing the communication skills in this book you will improve your leadership qualities. You will need to be assertive so as to be able to persuade group members to act in the way you consider best for the group.

Developing your interpersonal skills will help you to become an effective group leader even though you may not have been born one!

DEVELOPING GROUPS

Groups are much more easily developed if their members are not separated by long distances and have similar personalities and characteristics.

The more that attitudes are held in common, the better the group is likely to function.

Research undertaken by B W Tuckman in 1965 ('Developmental Sequence in Small Groups', *Psychological Bulletin*, 63, pp 384–99) suggests that groups pass through four stages of development:

FORMING $\Rightarrow$ STORMING $\Rightarrow$ NORMING $\Rightarrow$ PERFORMING

Forming – This is a 'testing the water' phase during which group members spend time establishing the reactions of other members to themselves and to the tasks and responsibilities to be carried out.

Forming is an important stage of group development in that it helps to set the standards of behaviour to which the group conforms.

Each group member tries to:

- create a favourable first impression by dress and manner;
- communicate with other members of the group;
- listen to what other members of the group are saying; and
- assert influence on the decision-making process.

Storming – Soon after formation, conflicts arise as group members argue about how power and status will be divided within the group. Some might think a leader should be elected. Some might seek a more democratic approach and others might want a combination of both approaches.

At this difficult stage of development you will need to:

- use your negotiating skills to help resolve conflicts;
- use your problem-solving skills, offering alternative solutions to resolve differences of opinion so that decisions may be made; and
- communicate effectively and assertively but try not to be too insistent on getting your own way – you may be able to bring other group members round to seeing things your way at a later stage.

Norming – As soon as the initial conflicts within the group are resolved, the group can settle down and begin to work efficiently. Individuals will accept their agreed responsibilities and procedures that need to be established are put in place. The group is now ready to undertake its tasks and activities.

Performing – Now that each group member is working for the good of the group, rather than for his own benefit, the group can concentrate on attaining its aims and objectives.

Not all groups will adhere exactly to the four stages outlined above but most will follow a similar development process. Understanding how groups work is important for members of any group. Groups are made up of individuals. They are dynamic. Each group member will influence the group by bringing knowledge, experience, skills, personality and attitude, all of which will help the group to function.

All the communication, personal and interpersonal skills in this book will assist you in working well within a group.

After each group encounter, assess your performance within the group. Ask yourself:

- Did I carry out my individual responsibilities/tasks to the best of my ability?
- Was my contribution in the best interests of the group, or did I let my individual aspirations get in the way?
- How can I best serve the interests of the group in the future?

5

Written Communication Skills

Although most driving instruction is given verbally you will on occasion have to use the written word. This chapter covers the Practical Teaching Skills required when:

- preparing hand-outs;
- giving written feedback;
- recording students' progress;
- designing visual aids; and
- writing business and promotional letters.

To ensure quality you need to consider a number of common points which apply to nearly all forms of written material:

- the style of writing and the words used should match the ability and level of understanding of the recipient;
- what you have written should be grammatically correct;

- the writing, whether typed or handwritten, should be neatly and legibly presented; and
- before being distributed, the written material should be carefully checked for correct spelling and terminology.

5.1

PREPARING HAND-OUTS

Hand-outs are most commonly used to support verbal communication by:

- reminding the student of the key points of a topic;
- reinforcing the information given verbally;
- referring the student to points which are difficult to communicate verbally; and
- acting as a promotional tool for your business or organisation.

The DESIGN of the hand-out is crucial. It should:

- focus on the KEY POINTS – the reader may totally disregard a long essay;
- where appropriate, include diagrams, pie charts, graphs etc, particularly if statistics are included; and
- be typed or professionally printed.

In addition to thinking about the design of hand-outs, you should also consider WHEN to give them out.

- Hand-outs distributed BEFORE the lesson or presentation can act as a guide to the student, directing the flow of topics (rather like an agenda). This can cause a problem if the student reads the hand-out but doesn't listen to or watch the presentation.
- Hand-outs distributed AFTER the lesson or presentation might not be read at all as the recipient feels that he has already heard all he needs to know about the topic covered.

A useful compromise would be to distribute the hand-out DURING the lesson or presentation but, to prevent this from becoming a distraction, you should:

- stress that the hand-out is to be used after the lesson or presentation; or
- give the student time to read the hand-out before continuing with the lesson or presentation; then
- ask the student to put the hand-out away before continuing with the lesson or presentation.

By following the above points, you should be able to maintain the attention of the student.

In a one-to-one lesson, it is often best to give the hand-out at the end of the lesson but set a task for the next lesson which involves the pupil in studying the hand-out. For example:

'The hand-out explains how the three foot controls work and the words I am going to use when dealing with them. On the next lesson I am going to test you on your understanding of them.'

This will help to keep the pupil's interest in between lessons by stimulating activity and involvement.

5.2

WRITTEN FEEDBACK

Most of the guidelines for giving verbal feedback are valid when giving written feedback for your students (see chapter 3).

When teaching on a one-to-one basis, or in small groups, it is useful for the students to be given written feedback at the end of each lesson or training session. The purpose of the feedback is to let the student know what has been done well and what areas need improvement.

A simple 'duplicating' book can be used, the top copy being given to the student, the bottom copy being kept by the instructor for reference.

Written feedback should be given in a sensitive way. You should adopt the following rules.

- Always be positive. Don't just tell the student what needs improving; give encouragement when needed and praise for what has been done well.

- Give some encouragement before any criticism.
- Give feedback in a helpful way rather than judgmental. For example, instead of 'You will fail your test if you drive jerkily', it is better to write 'Your passengers will feel much more comfortable if you give them a nice smooth ride, so try to use the foot controls more smoothly'.
- Only offer feedback on things that are controllable. Telling the pupil that the reason he cannot reverse in a straight line is that he is not turning round in the seat enough because he is too fat will not solve the problem.
- Don't give criticism without offering a remedy for the problem.
- Include in the feedback, tasks to be carried out in between lessons/training sessions as a way of preparing the student for the next lesson.

5.3

RECORDING STUDENTS' PROGRESS

Keeping a record of the pupil's or trainee's progress is important in that it allows both the teacher and the student to monitor which skills have been mastered and which need further work. It could be as simple as using a card index system or as complicated as storing the information required on a computer database. This will vary depending on the type of training given, the size of the organisation and the number of students involved.

One of the biggest problems for learners when they first start their lessons is that they have a feeling of insecurity, largely due to their not being able to compare their progress (or lack of it) with that of their peers who may also be learning to drive.

Although we are teaching driving as a *life skill*, the system of giving our pupils a series of objectives related to the requirements of the driving test or the recommended syllabus for learner drivers helps to overcome this problem.

We have already covered 'TEACHING BY OBJECTIVES' in section 4.1. On the same lines, there is no reason why you should not devise a progress chart for your pupils which links in with the course objectives, thus killing two birds with one stone. Both you and your pupil can then see how much progress is being made against the requirements of the L test itself.

Using this system would also give you an instant reminder of which particular topic is the next one to be covered during the lessons.

It is also helpful when pupils are switched from one instructor to another, such as in the event of the instructor being ill or on holiday, or if the pupil has moved to another area.

Provided the new instructor is given the progress chart, he can pick up where the previous instructor has left off.

The best way to implement this system would be to include the pupil's progress chart on the appointment card, and for the instructor to keep a separate master copy in the car. Progress sheets could be put on a clip-board in alphabetical order by surname so that objectives, when attained, can be crossed off the list.

A typical list of objectives, which could double as a progress chart is shown below:

Valid driving licence		Act properly at road junctions	
Eyesight test		Mirror(s) signal approach to junctions (MSMPSL)	
Introduction to car and controls		Position/speed/awareness	
Pre-starting drill		— position vehicle correctly before turning right/left	
Starting up and moving off			
Slowing down and stopping		— avoid cutting right hand corners	
Make proper use of the accelerator		Overtake/meet/cross path of/other vehicles safely	
clutch			
gears		Position vehicle correctly during normal driving	
footbrake		Allow adequate clearance to stationary vehicles	
handbrake		Take appropriate action at pedestrian crossings	
steering		Select a safe position for normal stops	
Move away/safely/under control		Show awareness and anticipation of the actions of/pedestrains/cyclists/drivers	
Moving off up/down hill/at an angle		Approaching — roundabouts	
Stop vehicle in an emergency promptly/under control		— crossroads	
Reverse into a limited opening left or right under control/with due regard to others		— traffic lights	
		— pedestrian crossings	
Turn round by means of forward/reverse gears/under control/with due regard to others		— one-way streets	
		Speed appropriate	
Make effective use of mirror(s) well before:		Overtaking moving vehicles	
Take effective rear observation well before:		Anticipation	
— signalling		Driving in heavy traffic	
— changing direction		Pupil taking the initiative	
— slowing down or stopping		More difficult manoeuvres	
Give signals where necessary/correctly/in good time		Highway Code questions	
Take prompt and appropriate action on all:		Parking	
— traffic signs		Competence at junctions etc.	
— road markings		Speed/lane positioning in line with conditions	
— traffic lights		Practice test requirements	
— signals given by traffic controllers		Ready for Test?	
— other road users		Post-test lessons	
Exercise proper care in the use of speed		Motorway driving	
Make progress by avoiding undue hesitancy		Advanced Driving Test	
— driving at speed appropriate to road/traffic conditions			

Progress chart

5.4

DESIGNING VISUAL AIDS

One of the ways of bringing your lesson or presentation to life is to use visual aids. Carefully designed visual aids offer you a number of benefits:

- they add structure to the presentation;
- they make it easier for your student to understand what you are saying by clarifying difficult concepts, detailing the position of your vehicle, other vehicles and other road-users in specific situations and showing how mechanical things work;
- they act as a memory prompt for you during your lesson or presentation, making it less likely that you miss anything important out;
- they are an effective way of communicating statistics or technical information; and
- they stimulate the interest of your pupil thus helping to maintain their attention.

Never forget that 75 per cent of all learning is through the eyes. And a picture paints a thousand words (provided it is a good picture!).

Visual aids usually fall into two categories: DIRECT AIDS and PROJECTED AIDS.

Most of the direct visual aids used in classrooms have been adapted for use in the car. The car IS your 'classroom' and visual aids will help you to create an environment where learning takes place. Projected aids have been covered in section 4.13 (Teaching in the classroom).

DIRECT AIDS can be either models or diagrams which may be either pre-prepared by you or made/drawn as the lesson progresses to suit the particular needs of the pupil or the circumstances.

Diagrams can be written on dry-wipe boards or flip pads, models can be used in conjunction with magnetic board lay-outs which allow you to recreate different traffic situations.

Visual aids can be used to display key words, mnemonics or phrases, summarise main points, and build up a routine step by step, thus helping the student to follow its development (eg, MSM becomes PSL becomes LAD).

Where possible, visual aids which are likely to be used frequently should be prepared in advance and designed with the following in mind.

- Do not OVERLOAD the visual aid with information. Keep it simple, using only KEY WORDS.
- Where KEY WORDS are used, make them large enough to be seen by those students who may need glasses for reading.
- Use different colours where possible to add to its appeal.
- Turn the visual aid sideways so that the student can see it – remember it is mainly for their benefit not yours!
- Make sure that you are not covering up the visual aid with your hand when pointing to key areas.
- Talk to the pupil, not the visual aid, and INVOLVE the pupil in using the visual aid. Ask questions to test their understanding of the KEY POINTS in the visual aid you are using.
- Once you have finished with the visual aid, put it away – USE IT then LOSE IT, otherwise it becomes a distraction.

The effectiveness of your visual aids is limited only by your ingenuity, improvisational skills, and how you design and use them.

5.5

WRITING BUSINESS AND PROMOTIONAL LETTERS

Driving instructors, because of the nature of the services they provide, get little practice in communicating in writing to customers, suppliers or business associates. You must, therefore, bear in mind the key guidelines.

> *Business or promotional letters should paint a clear picture of the person or organisation sending them.*

Business letters do not simply provide information. They create an image of the sender by the style of the letter heading, its typeface, and by the way in which it is composed and typed.

Business letters are also often 'legal documents', possibly committing the sender to a specific course of action. They can also convey technical information which, if incorrect, could lead to serious consequences for both the sender and the recipient.

Whether you are writing to the bank manager, the DSA, your customers, or anybody else in connection with business, you should carefully consider the purpose of the letter and the most suitable layout.

In this book we will concentrate on promotional letters.

PROMOTIONAL LETTERS

Any letter promoting your business should be designed to persuade the recipient to want to use your services, or recommend them to others.

A typical promotional letter should clearly inform the recipient about:

- the services being offered;
- where the services will be provided;
- the cost of the services;
- the duration of any training courses;
- the content of any training course (eg, if formal training is to be given, a syllabus should be included with the letter);
- any qualifications held by those providing the service;
- membership of any trade associations;
- any code of practice which is to be adopted; and
- any special benefits to be gained by using the services you are providing which may not be available from your competitors.

If the information you are giving is extensive and complicated, it might be better to send a short covering letter with a specially designed leaflet or brochure explaining the finer details of the services you are offering.

At a much simpler level, you might wish to write to all your previous customers, asking for referrals and recommendations to their friends or relatives.

At Christmas time, a card sent to all past and existing customers can often reap dividends by bringing in referrals. As this is a tax deductible expense anyway, you have everything to gain and little to lose.

6

Evaluating and Developing Your Personality and PTS

Some driving instructors have fairly limited Practical Teaching Skills and survive on personality alone. Others have very well developed PTS but lack the personality required to be really effective teachers of driving.

Just imagine how much more effective the instructor becomes when he has a good mix of the two!

By developing the PTS and other transferable personal skills in this book your self-assurance and self-confidence will improve. Situations that once seemed daunting, such as taking a check test, or formal presentations to groups of ADIs, will become enjoyable experiences in which you are happy to display your abilities to others.

For some instructors, these specific personal benefits will be more important than the wider career implications, especially for the more introverted individuals who shy away from social encounters.

Many driving instructors fall into this category. They sometimes are not keen to work with others and prefer to be left alone to 'do their own thing'. Many do not even choose to join any ADI association. It is probable that one of the reasons they chose to become driving instructors in the first place was that they would be left to work alone, at their own pace and in their own way.

This chapter should help you to develop your personality by improving the following:

> *Personal skills*
>   *– Assertive skills*
>   *– Affective skills*
>   *– Reflective skills*
> *Problem-solving skills*
> *Decision-making skills*

The development of the above will greatly enhance your teaching ability by making you more 'personable'. This, when combined with the other PTS, should result in you receiving more recommendations from existing and past pupils.

Your personality profoundly influences how you behave, react and feel towards others and towards difficult situations. How other people react and respond to you will be determined partly by your personality and the confidence that you display to others.

This is particularly so in the environment of driving instruction where you are dealing with others on a one-to-one basis or in small groups. Your pupils especially will look to you for advice and help.

People with similar personalities tend to work together more harmoniously. You should therefore try to adapt your personality to match that of each individual pupil.

Remember; to be able to teach Mary how to drive, you firstly have to know all about driving and, secondly, you have got to know all about Mary!

Knowing and understanding your personality, and being able to modify it to match that of the people you are dealing with will help you to interact more effectively with them.

Some instructors do this intuitively, without having to think about it.

Others have to work at improving the technique, just as they do with the other PTS.

Listed below are a number of words which describe various personality characteristics. Read through the list, ticking those which you recognise in yourself. Put a cross beside those that you think do not describe yourself.

Adaptable	Aggressive	Amiable	Aloof
Ambitious	Argumentative	Assertive	Caring
Cheerful	Confident	Considerate	Creative
Decisive	Defensive	Dependable	Determined
Easy-going	Emotional	Enthusiastic	Extrovert
Fickle	Flexible	Forceful	Friendly
Gregarious	Hard-working	Honest	Humorous
Inconsiderate	Mild-mannered	Obstinate	Open-minded
Orderly	Over-cautious	Persistent	Reliable
Reticent	Self-conscious	Shy	Sincere
Systematic	Tactful	Tenacious	Trustworthy

When you have done this, look at the personality traits you have ticked and assess how you come across to your pupils. How do your friends think of you? Do they see you in the same way as your pupils do? Do they see you in the same way as you see yourself? Do they see you as being aloof, inconsiderate and over-cautious, or do they see you as being friendly, considerate and confident?

Ask three close friends to write down three words each which they think sum up your personality, then compare it with your own list and see how well they match up.

Consider how your pupils think of you. Do they see you in the same way as your friends do? This analysis should help you to see yourself as others see you.

6.1

PERSONAL SKILLS

Personality development is dependent upon improving your assertive, affective and reflective skills.

The development of these will in turn help you to strengthen two other skills which you use every day of your working life: PROBLEM-SOLVING SKILLS and DECISION-MAKING SKILLS.

In chapter 4 we have mentioned that the instructor must be able to persuade his learners to do whatever it is that he wishes them to do in the way that he wants them to do it. Persuasion is not only necessary when dealing with the pupil's control of the vehicle and road procedure but also when handling other problems which may arise from time to time, such as unreasonable requests from the pupil.

In dealing with these situations the instructor needs to use his ASSERTIVE SKILLS and his AFFECTIVE SKILLS.

ASSERTIVE SKILLS

Assertiveness is the art of using clear and direct communication in order to get people to do what you want them to. When dealing with pupils you will need to be assertive, but in a friendly and sensitive way, sometimes with safety in mind. Being assertive enables you to:

- Be direct and ask for what you want;
- say 'no' clearly and firmly without causing offence and embarrassment; and
- take responsibility or control, sometimes against the wishes of your pupil.

Some instructors are naturally assertive while others are more reticent and find it difficult to say 'No', or refuse unreasonable requests. If you are a non-assertive individual you need to realise that being assertive does not involve aggression, but simply firmness.

There are many situations where the instructor needs to be assertive, for example making a request of the pupil which they might see as being unreasonable;

'Julie, I would like you to consider postponing your test!'

coping with the refusal of a request;

'If you don't postpone the test Julie, I will not be able to let you use the school car as you are not safe!'

refusing a request yourself;

'I'm sorry John, but you are not yet ready to put in for the driving test. You need to make a bit more improvement.'

apologising;

> 'I'm sorry that you feel you want to change instructors, but if I let you go on test when you are still unsafe the examiner will not be very pleased and you may have an accident. If you don't trust my judgement then perhaps it *would* be better if you do find another instructor!'

The easiest way to be assertive without causing offence is to be: FACTUAL, POSITIVE, PERSUASIVE and PERSISTENT.

One way of helping to overcome difficult situations is to clearly state your 'trading terms' on the pupil's appointment card. For example:

Cancellations – Unless 24 hours' notice is given, lessons will be charged for.

The school cannot be held responsible for postponement of the test due to bad weather or illness of the examiner.

Your instructor is one of the best trained in the profession and you should be guided by him/her regarding your readiness for the test. Your instructor will advise you when you should apply for the driving test.

The school car is available for driving tests, at the discretion of the instructor and subject to regular lessons being maintained.

In the interests of road safety, the school car may be withdrawn from the driving test if, at the discretion of the instructor, the pupil is considered to be unsafe.

The simple provision of the above on the appointment card will lessen the chances of arguments of this nature by adding weight to the instructor's words. In the eyes of the pupil the decision becomes 'company policy' and not just the whim of the instructor. The fact that the instructor may be 'the company' is neither here nor there.

Being assertive in a sensitive way will be easier to achieve if you develop your AFFECTIVE SKILLS.

AFFECTIVE SKILLS

AFFECTIVE in this context refers to your feelings and emotions, your attitudes and values, and how these 'affect' your interpersonal relationships.

Often, how successfully you deal with people and problems is determined by how you are feeling at the time, and your attitude towards the person or problem you are dealing with.

When dealing with other people, always try to:

- Treat them with respect. Even though you may be feeling low, do not release your frustrations on them. Try to control any 'mood swings' you may have.
- Be sensitive to their feelings and problems. Try not to offend people by what you say and how you say it. Get their side of the story and listen carefully to what they say. Respect their feelings but help them to see your side of the story.
- Be polite. Do not be rude or expect them to be servile. Treat them as you would wish to be treated yourself.
- Be sympathetic. Show concern for their well-being. Learn to pick up both verbal and non-verbal signals which may indicate their concern. Make time to find out what the cause of their concern is and provide sympathy and support when needed.

Look for and consider alternative solutions. For example, 'Could you manage to fit in some extra lessons in order to correct the problems you are having with emerging at junctions so that you are safe enough to take the test? Perhaps you could get some extra practice with your family.'

When confrontations of this nature do occur, always analyse the way you dealt with the situation. Ask yourself whether you did everything possible to work out alternative solutions to the problem. How did the pupil react to your handling of the situation?

In this respect, you are likely to learn more from your mistakes than you will from your successes and the experience gained will help you to overcome similar problems in the future!

Your development of problem-solving skills (covered later in this chapter) will lessen the likelihood of you facing the type of situations we have dealt with in this section.

REFLECTIVE SKILLS

REFLECTIVE SKILLS can be used first of all to evaluate how your personality might be modified to make you more personable, and secondly to measure how well your PTS are developing.

When you reflect upon your current activities and interests, so as to be able to build on your strengths and develop your weaknesses, you need to be objective and use a systematic approach.

> *Only by painting yourself a clear picture of your character and personality will you be able to assess where your strengths lie and your weaknesses exist.*

In this section we will be showing you how to use your reflective skills to develop your personality. As a starting point you need to reflect upon:

- current activities (other than giving lessons); and
- other interests and hobbies.

Current activities
To evaluate your current activities so as to establish where your strengths lie, begin by listing those activities that you frequently undertake. Try to be objective when completing the table, an example of which is shown below.

Column one shows the ACTIVITY; column two shows the SKILLS REQUIRED; and column three shows how you RATE your ability in using the skills which are required. Use a bi-polar marking system similar to that used by the SE/ADI on the check test: 1 – being not competent in your use of the skill in question; 2 – having some competence; 3 – being fairly competent; 4 – being very competent: 5 – being expert at using the skill.

Activities	*Skills required*	*Rating*
Involvement at local ADI association meetings	Working with groups Leading others Conversational skills Planning events Assertiveness Affective skills	
Attending local SEs meetings	Note taking skills Listening skills Thinking skills Questioning skills	

Parent/teachers	Committee skills
association	Communication skills
or other	Negotiating skills
committee work	

Other interests and hobbies

Like your activities, your interests and hobbies also give you an insight into how well you use your personal skills. By analysing what you like doing, and the skills involved, you can shed light on your potential capabilities.

For example, if you enjoy playing football it might be because you get pleasure from competing against others (an enterprising skill), that you like to study other players' styles of play (requiring assessment skills), or that it gives you a sense of achievement in trying to improve your performance (a personal skill).

Your interest in football may be less in the game itself and the result of the match than in the satisfaction you derive from playing the game.

List your interests and hobbies with those you most enjoy at the top and those you least enjoy at the bottom. In the second column, state explicitly the skills you use successfully in each of the interests, and in the third column give an evaluation of your skill – 1 being low, 5 being high.

For example, you might write something like this:

Rank order of interests	*Skills required*	*Rating*
1 Playing cards	Intellectual skills	4
	Verbal communication skills	2
	Reading body language	5
2 Reading novels	Reading skills	5
	Intellectual skills	3
3 Windsurfing	Dexterity skills	5
	Physical skills	5

Taking the above example, a picture emerges of an individual with interests that require little interaction with others. The skills that have been identified and assessed are very much INTRAPERSONAL rather than INTERPERSONAL. This would indicate that in order to develop a more balanced portfolio of skills, this person needs to seek interests that involve much more interaction with other people, such as team sports, activity clubs and perhaps local ADI associations!

6.2

PROBLEM-SOLVING SKILLS

In driving instruction, problem solving often needs to be carried out without the usual amount of time that one has when solving problems in other environments.

When problems do arise, decisions often have to be taken immediately, sometimes with safety in mind.

Solving problems usually involves transferring knowledge and understanding stored in the long-term memory to new situations.

The good instructor will, if time allows, involve the pupil, working together to solve the problem. The function of the instructor is to 'guide' the pupil towards solving the problem; presenting alternatives for consideration by the pupil and asking thought provoking questions which will help the pupil to shed light on the problem being considered.

If your pupils can, with your help, solve problems, they will be better able to understand why the problem arose in the first place, and how similar problems could be prevented in the future.

The systematic approach of following a series of stepping stones, should lead the pupil to identifying the different options available, and eventually to the most feasible solution to the problem.

If any of the steps are missed out, then it is unlikely that the pupil will arrive at the best solution. As each problem will be slightly different from the last, not all problems can be treated alike.

> *You must use your critical thinking skills to ensure that the pupil considers all the options, arrives at the best solution, and successfully implements that solution.*

Problem solving invariably precedes DECISION MAKING.

6.3

DECISION-MAKING SKILLS

The purpose of PROBLEM SOLVING is to discover what caused a particular situation, so that you may use the knowledge to DECIDE exactly how to deal with the problem.

A key element in DECISION MAKING is that of ASSESSING and BALANCING risk.

For example, a partly trained pupil is approaching a traffic light which has been green for some time. Following your instructions, the pupil slows the car down to such a speed that he can stop if necessary. Your car is just coming up to the line and the traffic light changes to amber. You know that the pupil could, and should, stop at the line, but there is a big lorry travelling much too close behind you. It's DECISION TIME!

You need to BALANCE the risk and because you don't have time to consult with your pupil, you probably say something like 'Keep going!' or 'Don't stop!' Had you said nothing then your pupil would probably have stopped suddenly with disastrous consequences.

In this sort of situation, where you have overridden a decision by the pupil, you would then need to stop somewhere safe and discuss what happened with your pupil. You would need to explain to the pupil why his decision was overridden by you.

The usual steps in the decision-making process are:

1. specifying your aims;
2. reviewing the different factors;
3. determining the possible courses of action;
4. making the decision; and
5. implementing the decision.

This is fine under normal circumstances and when making business decisions for example, but when you are travelling along the road and situations are developing quickly, you need to simplify the process to

$$\text{LOOK} \Rightarrow \text{ASSESS} \Rightarrow \text{DECIDE} \Rightarrow \text{ACT}$$

> *The instructor's function is to transfer the ability to make almost immediate decisions, using the LADA process, to the pupil as soon as possible, but being prepared to OVERRIDE decisions taken when safety is in question.*

The sooner your pupils are making decisions for themselves, the sooner they will be ready to drive unaccompanied.

For most pupils, the first time they will ever drive 'unaccompanied' is on the driving test, where the examiner should not be giving any verbal assistance to the pupil driving. Before this, a good way to introduce decision making to the pupil, and to test his ability to make decisions, is to let him drive home towards the end of the lesson, giving no instructions or directions, except where unplanned situations arise and safety is in question.

Everybody makes mistakes, and when bad decisions have been made, either by you or your pupil, they should be analysed. You will both learn more from your mistakes than you will from your good decisions!

6.4

PTS EVALUATION AND DEVELOPMENT

This section will show you how to evaluate your skills, achievements and satisfactions. This will assist you in deciding how best to continue your personal and career development. To be able to evaluate your PTS you must use your REFLECTIVE SKILLS because much of the work involved in developing your PTS has to be done by yourself.

> *You need to recognise your strengths, analyse your weaknesses and implement a self-development programme. This reflection process requires you to be objective and to use a systematic approach.*

You should consider the following:

- the PTS you are currently using;

- your achievements; and
- your satisfactions.

THE PTS YOU ARE CURRENTLY USING

To bring all the previous chapters together, you need to draw up a 'master list' of PTS, similar to that given below, which you can use to analyse and evaluate your levels of competence and decide which PTS you need to improve.

To analyse how well you are using your portfolio of PTS, mark against the list how well you think you are doing. Use the following rating scale to indicate your level of ability.

1 – Not very good and requiring considerable improvement.
2 – Some basic ability but with need for improvement.
3 – Not bad, but scope for improvement.
4 – Reasonably competent, slight room for improvement.
5 – Highly competent, scope for fine tuning.

PTS used while giving driving lessons   *Your Skill Rating (1–5)*
Verbal communication
Giving instructions
Giving directions
Giving explanations
Use of visual aids
Giving demonstrations
Own driving ability
Transferring knowledge
Transferring understanding
Transferring attitudes
Skill training
Question and Answer techniques
Giving feedback
Gaining feedback
Listening skills
General appearance
Using positive body language
Reading the body language of your pupils
Giving encouragement when needed

PTS used while giving driving lessons	Your Skill Rating (1–5)
Giving praise when deserved	
Affective skills	
Assertive skills	
Being patient	
Being sympathetic	
Sounding enthusiastic	
Putting the pupil at ease	
Problem-solving skills	
Decision-making skills	
Recapping at the start of the lesson	
Lesson planning	
Teaching by objectives	
Clearly stating the objectives for the lesson	
Selling ideas and concepts	
Matching the level of instruction to the ability of the pupil	
Flexibility in being able to change the lesson plan if necessary	
Route planning	
Use of simple and unambiguous language	
Transferring responsibility to the pupil	
Fault recognition	
Fault analysis	
Fault correction	
Timing of fault recognition and analysis	
Use of verbal intervention	
Use of dual controls	
Testing skills	
Recapping at the end of the lesson	
Linking forward to the next lesson	
Setting tasks for in between lessons	
Use of role-play skills (if relevant)	

When you see a list of all the skills which you may use every day of your working life without even thinking about them, it will help you to realise just how important the job of teaching someone safe driving as a life skill really is. Perhaps we should all be charging more than we do for the services that we provide!

Verbal communication skills	*Rating (1–5)*
Use of different tones of voice when speaking	
Use of emphasis when speaking	
Use of figurative language	
Use of humour	
Use of pronunciation	
Use of pitch	

Non-verbal communication skills	*Rating (1–5)*
Use of positive body language	
Use of appropriate dress	
Interpreting the body language of the learner	
Listening skills	

Written communication skills	*Rating (1–5)*
Written feedback for pupils/trainees	
Recording pupils'/trainees' progress	
Promotional and business letters	
Hand-outs	
Design of visual aids	

Personality development	*Rating (1–5)*
Assertive skills	
Affective skills	
Reflective skills	
Problem-solving skills	
Decision-making skills	

Group work skills	Rating (1–5)
Classroom management	
Leading a group	
Developing a group	
Working in a group	

If we say that a grade 4 or 5 is acceptable, and 3 or below is unacceptable, we now know which skills need to be developed.

A good starting point for improvement would be to re-read the sections in this book dealing with any of the above mentioned skills for which you have given yourself 3 or less.

You will then need to exercise self-determination or consider seeking professional help to improve the areas of weakness which you have identified. At the end of each lesson analyse your performance to see whether you think you have made improvement.

YOUR ACHIEVEMENTS

Many driving instructors tend to measure their achievements against how many pupils they get through the driving test first time. For the instructor who is serious about personal and career development, we need to look a bit further than that.

Your achievements do not have to have made the headlines, but may simply be successes about which you feel pleased.

A useful starting point would be to list all of your achievements that you consider are important. They need not be connected only with your job, but could include achievements in your social life. Emphasise those achievements that you found difficult to attain.

When you have completed your list, evaluating the PTS you have used in gaining the achievements will give you some insight into your strengths and weaknesses.

For example, your list could look something like this:

Achievement	PTS used	Rating
Teaching a deaf person to drive	Use of visual aids	5
	Demonstration skills	5
	Flexibility	5
	Patience	4
	Being sympathetic	4
	Setting between-lesson tasks	5
Winning the football competition	Teamworking	4
	Physical skills	5
Achieving a Grade 6 check test	Articulation	4
(The SE's comments should help	Enthusiasm	3
you to rate each component skill	Encouragement	4
used during the check test)	Friendliness	5
	Patience	5
	Self-confidence	4
	Objectives clear	5
	Level of instruction suitable	5

	Instructions easily understood	5
	Simple language used	4
	Q/A techniques	5
	Recap at the start	3
	Recap at the end	5
	Faults identified	5
	Fault analysis attempted	5
	Fault analysis correct	4
	Remedial action	4
	Timing of fault assessment	3
Cardington Grade A pass (Special driving test)	Driving skills	5

The person profiled above is able to accept pressure and to work well with others. To achieve examination/test success the individual must have prepared himself well which required self-discipline. You could summarise this person as being determined and dedicated.

YOUR SATISFACTIONS

Your self-awareness will be enhanced by evaluating your satisfactions. Everyone obtains satisfaction from some activity in which they participate. Listed below is a range of PTS. Against each skill you can indicate in the second column the level of satisfaction gained when using it. In the third column you can rate your skill level.
Your own list could look something like this:

PTS	Gain	Rating
Chairing meetings	satisfaction	4
Attending meetings	satisfaction	3
Leading others	satisfaction	4
Working with others	dissatisfaction	2
Taking decisions	satisfaction	3
Solving problems	satisfaction	5
Making formal presentations	dissatisfaction	1
Selling	dissatisfaction	2
Writing letters	dissatisfaction	2

Keeping accounts	dissatisfaction	2
Conversing with friends	satisfaction	5
Conversing with strangers	dissatisfaction	2
Using positive body language	satisfaction	4
Reading body language	satisfaction	5

Although the above list is not exhaustive or typical it may give you some ideas for compiling your own. By deciding whether or not you gain satisfaction by using your PTS you will gain insight into where some of your strengths lie and which weaknesses need to be overcome.

> *By developing your weakest PTS and reflecting on your achievements and satisfactions, you will most certainly become a better driving instructor.*

You are also likely to become more personable which should result in you getting more recommendations and improving your social life as well.

Change and development do not come overnight, however, and you should treat each new business and social encounter as an opportunity to experiment, practice, experience and reflect. If you are doing the same thing now that you were doing five years ago, you are probably doing something wrong! Development is a lifelong challenge but one which is well worth accepting for those brave enough to try.

7

Preparing for the Approved Driving Instructor Examination

This chapter is aimed primarily at those studying for the Approved Driving Instructor (ADI) examination. However, it should also give practising driving instructors an idea of the degree of knowledge required, the standard of driving and the level of instructional ability now needed by those wishing to become instructors.

For potential ADIs this chapter should help you to:

- develop your study skills;
- acquire sufficient knowledge and understanding to pass the Part 1 theory test;

- raise your standard of driving in order to be able to pass the Part 2 test of driving ability; and
- develop your Practical Teaching Skills (PTS) in order to be able to pass the Part 3 test of instructional ability.

Many existing ADIs have never taken a written examination nor a driving test at the current Part 2 standard. Some will not have taken the current Part 3 examination. This chapter should, therefore, be useful in helping those who have been qualified for a long time to measure their own level of knowledge, driving and instructional ability against the minimum entry standards for new instructors coming into the industry.

In recent years the Check Test has been made more compatible with the ADI Part 3 instructional ability test. It should be helpful for experienced instructors about to take a check test to compare the similarities between the two.

The Cardington special test has been made available to all ADIs. Every experienced instructor who has never taken an advanced driving test should carefully consider proving their driving expertise by taking this one.

If you think you know it all, you will probably not be reading this book. If, however, you think you may have something to learn, then read this chapter with an open mind.

Many questions are asked at local Supervising Examiners' (SE) meetings, national conferences and seminars which indicate that some experienced instructors probably know less than many of the newly qualified ADIs.

> *You owe it to yourself to make sure that your knowledge, driving technique and teaching methods are completely up to date.*

Provisional Driving Instructors (PDIs) will be encouraged to know that, once they have qualified, they will be able to compete confidently with the more experienced instructors in their area. If their training has been good, they will be equipped with the latest knowledge relevant to driver education, driving techniques and modern teaching methods.

7.1

___

THINKING ABOUT BECOMING AN ADI

Contrary to what you may think, driving instruction is not an easy job! Sitting beside different people and riding around in the sunshine in a new car may, to the outside observer, look like a 'doddle'. However, before committing yourself to a considerable outlay in terms of money, time and effort, you should seriously consider whether you will be suited to the job of giving driving instruction.

Initial training for the job involves a lot of hard work. When you have qualified you will need enormous patience, the stamina of a long-distance runner and total dedication. Your job will involve working unsociable hours and your concentration will need to be sustained at a high level at all times to protect you, your pupils and other road-users.

It is simply not enough to be able to provide yourself with a new car from a redundancy payment. Motivation is important. You must really want to do this type of work and not think of it as an easy option.

If you think you have the required qualities and decide that driving instruction is the job for you, you should go to a qualified tutor (someone who specialises in the training of driving instructors) who will give you an independent assessment. You will be advised on whether or not you have the potential to pass the examination and whether the job is likely to suit you.

7.2

___

THE PART 1 (Written Examination)

This book will help you to prepare yourself for the Part 1 (Written examination). In particular you will find chapters 2, 3 and 4 useful.

RESOURCE MATERIALS

The DSA recommend you to study and understand the following materials:

The Driving Instructor's Handbook (8th edn) by John Miller and Margaret Stacey, published by Kogan Page Limited, London, 1994. This is a training and reference manual for all driving instructors, especially those studying for the Part 1 Test of Theory.

The Driving Manual, published for the DSA by HMSO, London, 1992. This book is written to encourage the reader to learn and practice 'Safe driving for life'. It covers the skills required by those learning to drive and also gives advice to the experienced motorist. The need to develop correct attitudes and defensive driving techniques is emphasised throughout.

The Highway Code, prepared by the Department of Transport and the Central Office of Information for HMSO, London, 1993. This book of rules is issued with the authority of Parliament and contains important information for all road-users. It is designed to ensure that we all adopt the same rules in order to avoid accidents.

Your Driving Test, published for the DSA by HMSO, London, 1993. This book is aimed at those learning to drive or ride a motorcycle. It includes the officially recommended syllabus for learning to drive and is an essential teaching aid for driving instructors.

Driving Test Report (DL25A), issued by driving examiners to those failing the L Test. It is essential for driving instructors to be able to interpret the information given on this form in order to help their pupils correct weaknesses. You will find the form reproduced in *The Driving Instructor's Handbook.*

The Motor Vehicles (Driving Licences) Regulations 1987, published by HMSO. This document provides information on driving licence groupings and age limits for driving the different classes of vehicle. (Form D100 gives a summary and is available from main post offices.)

Instructional Techniques & Practice, by L Walklin, published by Stanley Thornes, Cheltenham, 1993. This book describes different types of techniques for teaching and assessing practical skills. In preparation for this test you are recommended to read and understand this book.

Know Your Traffic Signs, published by HMSO, London. This should supplement your knowledge of the purpose of the road signing system.

You should be familiar with the following forms:

- D1 – Application for a driving licence.

- V100 – Registering and licensing your motor vehicle.
  (The above two forms are available from main post offices.)
- DL26 – Application for a Driving Test: available at Driving Test Centres. You will need to be able to help your pupils to fill in their applications for the test.
- D10 – Driving Test Pass Certificate: issued by driving examiners to successful L Test candidates. You may have to assist your pupils with their application for a full licence, which will entail sending off this form. It is reproduced in *The Driving Instructor's Handbook*.
- ADI 26/PT Forms 1–10. These forms are issued by the SEADI at the end of the Part 3 Test of Instructional Ability. Reproduced in *The Driving Instructor's Handbook*, they show the areas assessed and the marks awarded for the two pre-set tests with a final grade for each Phase.

STUDYING TECHNIQUES

To be able to answer the questions correctly, you will need a thorough understanding of the information contained in the above materials. It is not enough just to read through them. You will find that some of the questions on the exam paper are worded negatively and will need some thought in working out the correct responses.

If you are preparing for this part of the exam at home, you may find that studying one subject at a time, in small doses, and then being tested on that material, can be the most effective way of understanding and retaining information. It is of little use reading a book from cover to cover if, when tested on the information a week later, nothing has been remembered.

To make it as effective as possible, your study must be planned and well organised. Section 2.5 outlines ways in which you can optimise your study time.

Trainees may purchase distance learning packs such as the structured home study programme written by Margaret Stacey. These are used by numerous instructor training establishments, and will help you to organise your study and take you step by step through the recommended reading materials.

If you feel there are too many distractions for you to prepare for this part of the exam at home, you may opt for one of the residential or other types of course. These should include a pre-course study programme with the necessary study and resource material.

However, although the main topics may be covered by your tutor in the classroom, you may find that you still have a great deal of private studying to do to get through all of the materials.

MULTIPLE-CHOICE EXAMINATION PROCEDURES AND TECHNIQUES

The Part 1 Test of Theory consists of an exam paper of 100 multiple-choice questions. You have to select the correct answer from the three given and you get an hour and a half in which to complete it. The following are examples of questions:

Q   Where should you not park your vehicle at night without lights?

A   (a)   Within 15 metres of a junction.
     (b)   On the right hand side of any road.
     (c)   On any road where the speed limit is 30 mph.

Q   The recommended following distance when travelling at 30 mph is:

A   (a)   75 feet.
     (b)   90 feet.
     (c)   60 feet.

Q   On a first lesson with a novice who has never driven before, the instructor should:

A   (a)   Insist on effective use of all of the mirrors.
     (b)   Ensure that the mirrors are all adjusted correctly.
     (c)   Not worry too much about the mirrors at this stage.

It may sometimes be relatively easy to eliminate an obviously incorrect answer straight away, but the two answers which remain may be very similar. Unless you have studied and *understood* the recommended reading materials, you may find it difficult to discriminate between these two.

You may also sometimes find it easier to work out which are the two incorrect answers in order to be left with the correct response. An example of this is:

Q Arm signals should be used:
A (a) Only when direction indicators are not working.
    (b) To reinforce direction indicators.
    (c) To help and warn other road-users, including pedestrians.

Answer (a) is incorrect because the word '*only*' invalidates it. There are other times when an arm signal would be useful.

Answer (b) is incorrect since it implies that arm signals should *always* be used to reinforce direction indicators.

Answer (c) is therefore correct because it positively confirms what *Highway Code* Rule number 45 states.

CHECKLIST OF KNOWLEDGE AND UNDERSTANDING REQUIRED TO PASS

To achieve the overall pass mark of 85 per cent you will need a thorough knowledge and understanding of all of the foregoing materials. The subjects are 'banded' in the examination paper and you must score at least 80 per cent in each of these bands to achieve a pass.

The subjects tested are banded as follows:

Band 1	Road procedure	25 questions
Band 2	(a) Traffic Signs and Signals	5 questions
	(b) Car Control	10 questions
	(c) Pedestrians	5 questions
	(d) Mechanics	5 questions
Band 3	(a) Driving Test	10 questions
	(b) Disabilities	5 questions
	(c) Law	10 questions
Band 4	(a) Publications	10 questions
	(b) Instructional Techniques	15 questions

ON THE DAY OF THE EXAMINATION

When you attend for the Part 1 exam, give yourself plenty of time to study the questions. Before selecting your answer, read each question at least twice to make sure you have understood it correctly. Only when you are happy that you have arrived at the correct answer should you mark your selection on the answer sheet provided.

If you have difficulty with answering any of the questions, leave these until you have answered all of those you are sure of. Then go through the question paper again, using a process of eliminating the incorrect alternatives so as to work out the *correct* answers. If you are still unsure, and if you have time available, it is worth having a guess at the correct answer. As you will not lose any more marks for an incorrect answer than you would for leaving it unanswered, at the end of the exam you should have answered *every* question.

Do not rush through the paper because others are leaving the room – they may have given up because they didn't study properly. Remember, you are given an hour and a half for a reason – so that you have sufficient thinking time!

Before the day of the examination make sure you are fully prepared to take and pass it!

Have you done enough studying? Do you fully understand all the forms, and the relevant parts of the recommended books? Do you understand the correct road procedures as covered in *The Driving Manual*? Will you be able to answer questions on basic car mechanics and vehicle maintenance? Do you fully understand the procedures for the L test? Will you be able to answer questions on instructional and teaching techniques?

7.3

THE PART 2 (Test of Driving Ability)

RESOURCE MATERIAL

The following publications should help you understand driving theory and the practices recommended by the DSA. They are desribed in more detail at the start of section 7.2.

- *The Driving Manual.*
- *The Highway Code.*
- *Know Your Traffic Signs.*
- *The Driving Instructor's Handbook.*

Another book which may help you to understand more about defensive driving techniques and assist in your preparation for the Part 2 Driving

Test is *The Advanced Driver's Handbook* (second edition) by Margaret Stacey, published by Kogan Page, London, 1995. It is a practical guide to safer driving. By combining established advanced and economic driving skills with defensive techniques, it provides drivers with a clearer insight into the locations at which accidents are likely to occur, the mistakes which precede them and the actions which should be taken to avoid them.

THE IMPORTANCE OF TRAINING

Even though you may have been driving for many years, and consider yourself to be highly experienced, you may have developed habits which detract from the overall efficiency of your personal driving skills.

Remember that this is a key stage in developing your career. It is well worth while, in terms of expense and effort, to be fully prepared for your Part 2 Test of Driving Ability. The standard of driving required for this test is extremely high. A failure will result from one serious or dangerous error or an accumulation of six minor errors. Hence, you cannot afford to make many mistakes!

The DSA set a limit of three attempts on this part of the exam so it is logical to be properly prepared before you take the first one. A failed exam will mean more expense and more pressure when you take it a second time! If you fail for a second time because you don't want to spend money on good training, your final attempt will be even more arduous.

Selecting a good trainer

It is no good trying to drive like a 'good learner'. Your personal driving skills need to be:

- brisk;
- safe;
- smooth;
- modern;
- courteous; and
- well controlled at all times, in all situations.

You may think it sufficient to have a couple of lessons with the local driving school because they have good pass rates at L test level.

However, the local driving instructor may have qualified a long time ago and may not be up to date with modern driving or training methods. To pass the ADI Part 2 requires a very high standard of driving and you do not want to be 'trained down' to L driver level.

An experienced trainer knows all about modern driving techniques and the standard required on this test. He will be able to show you how to bring your driving up to an efficient and effective level, eliminating any old habits which you may have developed. You may also have the benefit of seeing a good demonstration drive which should show you exactly what is required by the DSA.

Although you will not be asked to do this on your test, a good way to improve your planning and anticipation skills is to give yourself some commentary drives. A good trainer should be able to show you how this is done. Not only will it sharpen your awareness of what is happening all around, it will also be invaluable when you are teaching your pupils how to look ahead and anticipate what is likely to happen. In addition, it will get you used to translating actions into words – a major part of teaching someone how to drive.

The amount of training required will depend on your current standard of driving.

> *Listen to the advice given by your trainer. If you are not up to standard, put the test off until you are. Don't be ruled by how much it is costing – remember, it will cost you more if you fail, particularly if you fail your third attempt.*

WHAT THE EXAMINER IS LOOKING FOR

Your examiner will expect your driving to reflect a considerable level of experience.

> *You should be positive and confident. Your car should be seen to be an extension of yourself, with the controls being used smoothly and efficiently.*

Your driving should show that you understand the traffic rules and regulations laid down in the *Highway Code*. You should see and be prepared to act on all road signs and markings. Be aware of the speed limits for the road you are on.

Concentrate on what is happening all around you and work out the best way of dealing with each situation as it arises. You must be able to follow directions, keeping to routes in accordance with instructions given, and drive at correct speeds in relation to the road and traffic situations.

Routes used for the test

This test will normally include all types of roads – ie, urban and rural, with sections of motorway or dual carriageways. You should show that you are capable of of driving effectively in all conditions.

Wherever you live you should get plenty of practice at:

- driving in rural areas on country lanes and through villages;
- driving in busy towns and cities; and
- driving on motorways and dual carriageways.

To achieve a relatively fault-free drive you will need to display a sound attitude and expert control and handling of the vehicle, and be able to demonstrate your understanding of safe road procedure. Your attitude should be confident but caring. For example:

- Your personal driving skills should reflect your experience – do not try to drive like a learner.
- No matter who is sitting in your passenger seat, you should drive naturally and efficiently to suit the road and traffic conditions. Drive the way you know to be correct. Do not try to put on a special show for the examiner or try to analyse what he may be thinking – this will only distract you.
- If you realise you have made a mistake, try not to let it put you off. Forget what has happened and concentrate on what is happening now!
- Be positive at junctions and take any suitable opportunities to proceed safely, without taking chances and paying attention to all traffic signs and road markings.
- A courteous and patient attitude should be shown towards all other road-users. When in traffic queues, remember not to block pedestrian crossings, junctions or entrances.

- Anticipate the movement of pedestrians in busy areas and be ready to give way when appropriate, particularly near junctions. Your approach to pedestrian crossings should take into account all activity around them.
- Give cyclists plenty of room. If you cannot get past safely, hold back until you can.

Your use of all the controls should reflect your expertise and experience. For example:

- All controls should be used smoothly, avoiding pitch and roll faults.
- The gears should be smoothly engaged and appropriate to the vehicle's speed and selected to suit the road and traffic conditions.
- You should be selective in your use of the gears – remember, 'brakes are for slowing and gears are for going'.
- You should demonstrate good accelerator sense, avoiding unnecessary use of the footbrake.
- The handbrake should only be used when necessary – eg, for the longer waits and, particularly, where pedestrians are involved.
- An efficient steering method should be used at all times.
- The emergency stop may be carried out at a fairly high speed. Use the brake first, firmly but progressively. Consider the use of cadence braking in bad weather or if the road conditions are poor.
- You should be planning well ahead and anticipating events so that nothing has to be done in a rush or at the last moment.

The road procedure that you use should reflect your complete understanding of *The Driving Manual*. For example:

- Your road positioning and lane discipline on roundabouts and bends should be correct.
- Your use of all mirrors should be effective. The examiner will not be testing you on how many times you check them, but on how you respond to what you see by the decisions you make afterwards. You should be aware at all times of the movements of others.

- Give signals when they will help or warn any other road-user, including pedestrians. Avoid signals which will be of no benefit to anyone.
- Demonstrate your understanding of the different methods of signalling to road-users other than using the indicators – eg, early positioning, brake lights, eye contact, use of the horn when necessary.
- Use the MSM – PSL – LAD system of car control at all times.
- All of the manoeuvres should be carried out efficiently with particular attention being paid to observations throughout. If you are paying attention, no other road-user or pedestrian should appear without you knowing about it. You should respond correctly to what you see, by waiting when necessary.
- Effective observations should be made at all junctions, even when you may have priority – eg, at crossroads and traffic lights.
- When emerging at junctions, unless your zone of vision is excellent, use the CREEP and PEEP routine to edge forward until you can make a safe decision to proceed.
- On national speed limit roads, you should use your vehicle's capabilities to drive up to the speed limits when safe to do so. On motorways or dual carriageways, if safe, try to get your speed up to 70 mph in the acceleration lane – that is what it is designed for. When leaving this type of road try not to slow down while still on the main carriageway – that is what the deceleration lane is for.
- Show that you can compensate by driving at lower speeds when the road and traffic conditions dictate.

SOME COMMON REASONS FOR FAILING

One of the most common causes of failure of the Part 2 Test of Driving Ability is lack of progress. Being over-cautious demonstrates a lack of confidence. This fault is most common on dual carriageways and motorways.

Using the gears to slow the car down is the cause of many failures. The brakes should be used to provide time for working out whether it is safe to continue or whether a stop will be necessary. An appropriate gear should then be selected to suit the purpose. Making three un-necessary gear changes on the approach to a junction or hazard, often results in coasting as there is insufficient time in between changes to bring the clutch up. It also means that the left hand is not on the steering wheel as much as it could be when slowing down.

Other common reasons for failure are:

- loss of control in the emergency stop exercise;
- not making adequate observations or not responding to what is seen during the manoeuvring exercises;
- too high a speed in built up areas;
- causing inconvenience to other road-users;
- lack of discrimination when giving signals, using unnecessary or dangerous signals, timing signals incorrectly; and
- not taking effective observations before emerging at junctions.

Before you present yourself for the Part 2 test make sure you are fully prepared. Have you managed to raise your standard of driving to the minimum required to pass? Have you eliminated all serious faults, and are you driving briskly and smoothly? Have you had sufficient training to prepare you for the test?

ON THE DAY OF THE EXAMINATION

If you have had sufficient training and are properly prepared for this test, you should not be feeling too nervous about it. Get all of your documents ready the day before. You should take with you:

- your driving licence;
- a certificate of insurance;
- an MOT certificate if applicable; and
- the letter confirming your test appointment.

Although there is no legal requirement, it would be common sense to provide a rear view mirror for the examiner's use. It may be helpful to both of you if he can see situations behind which may have caused you to take defensive action. If you do decide to use one, make sure it is already correctly fitted in a suitable position before the examiner gets into the vehicle.

It will create a good impression if your car is clean, inside and out. It will also foster a professional image if you are smartly dressed for the occasion. You should aim at making the examiner feel comfortable with you even before you start the engine.

Ensure that your car is roadworthy. Check the tyres are properly inflated and have no defects, and that the lights, indicators and windscreen wipers are all working. Make sure that the washer bottle is topped up and that you have enough fuel.

Give yourself plenty of time to get to the test centre with a few minutes to spare. If you need to use the toilet allow time for this – remember, if you are uncomfortable it will affect your driving.

The result of this test is up to you and no one else. If you fail it will not be the examiner's fault – *you* will have failed yourself! You start with a clean sheet so try to keep it that way. Think positively and concentrate on your driving.

Good luck on your Part 2 Test of Driving Ability!

7.4

THE PART 3 (Test of Instructional Ability)

This section is not intended to be a short cut to passing the Part 3 examination. There is no short cut! What it will do, is to give PDIs all the information they require to be able to prepare themselves fully for what is the final hurdle in achieving their ambition of becoming an ADI. You cannot expect to learn how to teach someone the lifetime skill of driving simply by reading this or any other book. It must therefore be reiterated that there is no substitute for 'hands on' training with a professional tutor.

While the pass rate for candidates taking the Parts 1 and 2 exams is over 50 per cent, only 30 per cent of those taking the Part 3 examination manage to pass it. This indicates that many PDIs are taking the exam with inadequate preparation. However, if they are trained to teach driving as a lifetime skill, and can treat the supervising examiner as a real learner, passing the exam should be a formality.

With the limit of three attempts set on this part of the exam, it makes sense to be well prepared before you take the first one. As with the Part 2 examination, failure will mean more expense and more pressure when you take it for a second time.

If you fail on your third attempt, all the time and money you have spent up to that point will have been wasted. You will then have to wait two years from the date you passed the written exam before you can re-apply to begin the whole examination process again.

RESOURCE MATERIAL

To pass the Part 1 Test of Theory you had to do a lot of studying to learn and understand the theory of driving instruction. You now have to learn to put that theory into practice.

The PTS outlined in this book will give you a good foundation on which to build and develop your instructional ability. The book will also give you an understanding of what being a driving instructor is all about and help you to prepare for the Part 3 examination and for 'real lessons'.

You may need to refer to the following publications to reinforce your knowledge of how to teach in a properly structured manner.

The Driving Instructor's Handbook – refer to the chapters dealing with training for the Part 3, driver training and the driving test.

Your Driving Test – study the syllabus you will have to teach.

Learn to Drive in 10 Easy Stages by Margaret Stacey, published by Kogan Page, London, 1993. This book will assist you with structuring your lessons in easy, attainable steps. It will also give your students guidance on what to expect on their lessons and what to learn in between.

In-car Visual Teaching System published by Margaret Stacey, Auto-driva, Derbyshire. This visual aid will not only assist you with your explanations by serving as a 'memory jogger', it will also help your pupils to understand difficult concepts by showing them what you mean in picture format.

The ADI 14 Information Pack, published by the DSA, will tell you the format and content of the Part 3 examination.

THE PRE-SET TESTS (PSTs)

The Part 3 is a one-hour examination made up of two 'lessons' grouped into the following pre-set combinations. This means that any of the subjects listed on the left at Beginner phase or Partly Trained Phase will *always* be coupled with the Trained (Test Standard) Phase items listed on the right.

Phase 1 – Beginner

1. Controls
2. Moving off/stopping, use of mirrors

Phase 1 – Partly Trained

3. Turn in the road
4. Reversing (either right or left)
5. Emergency stop/use of mirrors (two separate subjects)
6. Pedestrian crossings/use of signals (two separate subjects)
7. Approaching junctions to turn right or left
8. T junctions – emerging

9. Crossroads
10. Meet, cross and overtake other traffic, allowing adequate clearance for other road-users and anticipation

Phase 2 – Trained

Crossroads

Meet, cross and overtake other traffic, allowing clearance for other road-users and anticipation

Approaching junctions to turn right or left

Emerging

Progress/hesitancy and general road positioning

Reverse parking

Pedestrian crossings/use of signals

Meet, cross and overtake other traffic, allowing adequate clearance for other road-users and anticipation

Pedestrian crossings/use of signals

Progress/hesitancy and general road positioning

The first 'lesson' is to be given to the SE playing the part of an absolute beginner or a pupil with a little knowledge. The second 'lesson' is to be given to the SE playing the part of a different pupil who has some experience and is at about test standard.

You will see that some subjects appear in both phases. It is extremely important that you can deal with these at the different levels required, adapting your level of instruction to suit the ability of the pupil you are teaching.

It is essential to note that in Phase 1 of pre-set test (PST) 01 and 02 you will be teaching somebody who has never driven before. You will probably have to drive the tuition vehicle to a suitable place before commencing the lesson. Similarly, when teaching one of the Phase 1 manoeuvres in PST 03 or 04 you will need to get the pupil to drive to a convenient place at which to carry out the manoeuvre.

In PST 10 (Phase 1) and PSTs 02 and 08 (Phase 2), the SE will nominate only two or three of the subjects listed. This is because it would be unreasonable to expect the PDI to cover all the subjects adequately in the 30 minutes allotted.

When teaching PST 05 (Phase 1) and PSTs 07 and 09 (Phase 2), remember that there are two separate subjects which need to be covered. It is not sufficient to cover the use of signals when dealing with pedestrian crossings. Similarly, when teaching PST 05 (Phase 1), it is not sufficient to teach the use of the mirrors in relation to carrying out the emergency stop exercise. The use of mirrors is a separate subject and must be treated as such. However, careful structuring of the lesson can link the two.

For example, you could deal with the mirrors first, and assess the pupil's use of them while driving to a suitable site for the emergency stop exercise. Then, when debriefing on the use of the mirrors, explain why the driver should always be aware of what is happening behind so that in the event of an emergency situation arising, he will be able to take account of following traffic.

As if the above is not enough to contend with, you will be dealing with an SE playing the part of two different learners with different personalities and characters. Not only will their level of ability be different but their characters could range from simple to complex. They may also have attitude problems which you will need to deal with.

Studying this book will be a good starting point, as it will give you some knowledge and understanding of all the PTS which make for good instruction. The PTS in this book will not only help you in the Part 3 examination but also when teaching learners when you have qualified.

However, reading this book is not enough. The complexity of this examination demands that you take specialist training with a qualified tutor or at an approved training establishment. Your local driving instructors may be excellent at teaching learner drivers. However, contrary to what they may think, it is unlikely that they will be able to train you to become a driving instructor unless they have had specialist training. This is because the skills required are totally different.

THE IMPORTANCE OF TRAINING

It is important to remember that, although you are training to take an examination, you are also training for a job which involves danger. To learn how to become a good instructor, you will need plenty of expert guidance.

No matter how well you know the subject material, putting it over in a way which will encourage learning to take place is a different matter altogether.

> *The modern driving instructor has to be a 'teacher', not just someone who rides around telling learners where to go and what to do. You will need to be able to teach your pupils to understand the why's and wherefore's involved in driving.*

A good trainer will be able to show you how to find out what your learner already knows, establish the 'base line' for the lesson and pitch the instruction to suit the ability and personality of that particular person.

Remember when selecting your trainer that you are investing in a career. Don't opt for what may appear to be the cheapest and shortest course. There are no short cuts!

A good tutor will train you to be able to cope with the complexities of teaching a wide range of subjects to an even wider range of pupils with different abilities, personalities and problems.

It is not essential to learn the PST subjects in pairs. What is required is a thorough understanding of the key points of each and the ability to be able to present the lesson at the appropriate level for the learner you are teaching.

Picking a good trainer

Even when going to trainers one has to be careful. Many ADIs giving training claim to provide 'easy ways' to pass the Part 3 test. But, there is no easy way. You can obtain sets of briefing notes which you will be told to memorise. The problem with memorising briefings and explanations is that as soon as your 'pupil' asks a question on the test it is likely to throw you completely.

Rather than learning briefings parrot fashion, it would be much more sensible to draw up a lesson plan for each of the PSTs. (An example is shown on pages 107–8.) This way you will be able to put your own personality into your teaching when you are explaining those objectives to your 'pupil'.

It is strongly recommended that you receive training either from a training establishment that is approved under the ADITE or DIARTE schemes (see chapter 9), or a specially qualified tutor. The associations representing driving instructors and schools of motoring, which are listed in the ADI 14 information pack, may be able to assist you in finding a good trainer. Many advertisements can be found in local and national newspapers, telling you how much money you can earn as a driving instructor. In some areas, there may be a shortage of good instructors, but a responsible trainer will be able to advise you on the situation in your own area.

Many PDIs fail the Part 3 because they find it difficult to treat the SE as a real learner. This is even more difficult if you have never taught a real learner! A good trainer will help you to overcome this problem by using role play and by showing you how to ask relevant questions. This is covered in more detail later in this chapter.

> *A few carefully chosen questions at the beginning of the lesson can prevent problems later on. The questions will need to be relevant to past experience or the new topic being taught.*

For example, if your 'pupil' has only had limited experience and is going to drive away from the test centre straight into traffic, you may need to ask: 'Do you normally drive away from here in your lessons?'. If the answer is 'No' you will need to ask: 'How do you feel about driving away from here?'.

If the 'pupil' says he would like to drive away from the test centre, you must be prepared to prompt him if traffic conditions are encountered which are beyond his level of competence.

It is difficult to ask your 'learner' realistic questions knowing full well that he is a supervising examiner who really knows a lot more than you do about the subject you are teaching.

This book will give you a good firm knowledge base of PTS. You will then need practical experience at presenting a lesson, putting your own personality into it asking questions to get the pupil involved and finding out what previous experience the 'learner' already has.

PRESENTING THE LESSON

This subject is covered in detail in section 3.2 but special allowances will need to be made for the short duration of each lesson on the Part 3.

A good starting point would be to know what the examiner is looking for on the test. Irrespective of whether you are teaching a novice, partly trained or test standard pupil, the lesson should include certain elements. These are: 1) Instructor characteristics, 2) Instructional techniques, and 3) Fault assessment.

Instructor characteristics

These should take account of the communication skills and PTS outlined in chapter 3. Instructor characteristics are personality traits and PTS which help you to communicate effectively with your 'pupil'. During the lesson, you will need to demonstrate your ability to be:

Articulate – speaking clearly so that your 'pupil' can easily understand what you are saying;

Enthusiastic – sounding as if you are genuinely interested in the topic you are talking about and in the 'pupil''s progress;

Encouraging – taking every opportunity to give your 'pupil' encouragement when needed;

Friendly – communicating in such a way that your pupil feels at ease and receptive to your instruction;

Patient – being prepared to repeat things or adapt what you are saying to help your 'pupil' understand what is required of them; and

Self-confident – sounding as if you are in control and know what you are talking about, which will help to give your 'pupil' greater confidence.

Instructional techniques

These are the PTS which help you to make learning more effective. They are all covered in more detail in chapters 3 and 4 and include:

- matching the level of instruction to the ability of the pupil;
- giving instructions which are easy to understand and unambiguous;
- using simple language and avoiding jargon and over-technical terms;
- giving feedback to the pupil as to how well he is doing and any improvements which may be necessary; and
- using verbal intervention and the dual controls as/when necessary.

Fault assessment

This is probably the most important category of PTS. As a professional driving instructor, in the interests of the safety and convenience of your 'pupil', yourself and any other road-users, faults must be accurately identified, analysed and corrected. You are strongly advised to study section 4.5 – Fault Assessment. On the Part 3 you must be able to demonstrate your potential ability to deal with faults with safety in mind.

You will need to pay particular attention to the following areas:

- Identifying faults made and dealing with them in a way which is appropriate to the seriousness of the fault;
- analysing the faults made – this should include what the 'pupil' did wrong, what they should have done and why it is important;
- finding time to correct faults made and offering remedial action; and
- timing the assessment of faults to best suit the needs of the 'pupil' – minor faults may be corrected on the move, whereas those of a more serious nature will need to be discussed as soon as a safe and convenient place can be found.

A good trainer will ensure that you fully understand the fault assessment techniques required on the test and that you can put them into practice. If further training is recommended, you would be well advised to take it.

The lesson plan will need to be varied to suit the level of ability of the 'pupil'. For example, if you are teaching the controls of the vehicle to a complete novice, the lesson will consist almost totally of a briefing and an explanation. Because of the time limit on the Part 3 it is unlikely that your 'pupil' will get the car moving whereas, when teaching a real pupil, you would make sure that they received some practical experience in moving off and stopping.

STRUCTURING THE LESSON TO THE TIME AVAILABLE IN THE EXAMINATION

This part of the ADI exam is designed to test your practical ability as an instructor – not your knowledge.

Your knowledge of the subject matter was tested in the Part 1 Test of Theory. Your skills at putting this knowledge into practice as a driver were tested on the Part 2 Test of Driving Ability. The Part 3 Test of Instructional Ability is to test whether you have the potential to teach new drivers the knowledge and skills required to survive on the roads.

The instructor is the manager of the environment and your job is to create an environment where learning can take place. You will therefore need to be aware of feedback from your 'pupil'. This feedback may be obtained:

- by using the question and answer technique;
- from body language;
- through improvement in performance.

Because of the limitations of time, avoid giving your 'pupil' a boring monologue which includes too much unnecessary detail of the subject, particularly if it takes so long to deliver that you have little time left for practical instruction.

Watch for body language from your 'pupil' such as fidgeting, yawning or looking at the watch. These may indicate that you need to get on with the practical part of the lesson.

A briefing should be what it says – BRIEF. Too often, too much time is spent in asking irrelevant questions and the lesson becomes almost an interrogation.

It is important that you accept what the SE says about what has already been covered on previous lessons. If you were teaching 'emerging at junctions' at Phase 1, a simple sequence of questions could be used to establish prior knowledge and understanding. For example:

'In your previous lessons, have you covered turning left and right into junctions?'

You would then need to listen carefully to the answer. If it is 'Yes', continue by asking:

'So, what routine procedure would you use when approaching these junctions?'

If the 'pupil' said, for example:

'Well my last instructor didn't really explain things to me in any detail',

you will then need to ensure that the 'pupil' fully understood about the MSM routine.

There will even be differences between the lesson plan for a partly trained pupil and that for a trained pupil. It will be helpful to you if we look at those differences.

LESSON PLAN FOR A PARTLY TRAINED PUPIL

An introduction – This should include introducing yourself to the pupil, and a couple of questions to establish how much knowledge and driving experience the pupil already has. You might also confirm how long it has been since the pupil has driven.

A briefing – This should include the key points of the topic to be taught and basic performance criteria.

The main body of the lesson – This may include an explanation of the lesson objectives, the EDP routine if appropriate, assessment, fault analysis, remedial action, feedback Q/A technique, visual aids and, where necessary, more practice and more feedback.

Because of the limitations of time, although the offer of a demonstration should be made, it might be more appropriate to give a talk-through instead. The best way in which to handle this is to give the 'pupil' the choice. You may even consider giving an explanation while demonstrating, for example for the 'turn in the road' exercise.

With a real pupil, you would probably include a recap at the start on what had been achieved in the previous lesson. You cannot do that on the Part 3 because, irrespective of which Phase the 'pupil' is at, you will be meeting for the first time. You should, however, still use the Q/A technique to 'set the scene'.

At the end of the lesson you would normally recap on what has been achieved during the lesson and link forward to what will be covered on the next one. Because the SE cuts you short before the lesson is completed, you may not be able to do this. Do not worry if the SE stops you 'in full flow'. This is purely because of the limitations of time.

LESSON PLAN FOR A TEST STANDARD PUPIL

Because the pupil may have already failed a test, or have a test coming up shortly, you will normally start with an assessment of how well the pupil is doing no matter what has been nominated as the topic for the lesson.

Listen carefully to the SE when he sets the scene for the lesson. As soon as you go into role and become the instructor, it is always a good idea to 'throw back' at your pupil any information given at the start by the SE. This helps to ensure that you are both on the same wavelength from the outset. You will need to include the following.

A briefing – Introduce yourself to the pupil and ask some questions to confirm what topic is going to be covered.

An explanation – Explain that an assessment will be given and what performance criteria you will be looking for.

An assessment drive – Watch carefully for any faults made by the pupil, correct minor faults on the move, give feedback, analyse more serious faults, and use visual aids or demonstrations if appropriate.

Offer remedial action – Do whatever is necessary to bring about improvement; such as prompted practice.

Debrief – Give more feedback and link forward to further instruction if required.

Many trainees acquire copies of the ADI 26 marking sheets. Remember that these are for the SE's use. Do not feel that you have to cover all of the items listed on the left-hand side and that you will automatically fail if you don't.

Remember you have to adjust the lesson to the time available. As long as you find out what the 'pupil' knows and cover the key points of what they don't know, you will be giving a good lesson.

You should ensure that, when the SE is on the move as the 'learner', all the correct safety procedures are followed. If they are not, then you must cover them and explain why they are important. Always relate to the safety and convenience of yourselves and other road users.

At all times you will need to be in control of your 'pupil'. Remember that the SE is human! He is likely to be asking himself from the learner's point of view:

- Have I gained knowledge I didn't have before the lesson?
- Have I gained understanding I didn't have before?
- Have I learnt new skills or improved existing skills?
- Has my attitude been modified by my driving instructor?

He is then likely to be asking himself:

- How much learning has taken place during the two lessons given?
- Would I recommend this instructor to a friend of the family?

TREATING THE EXAMINER AS A LEARNER

On the Part 3 exam the SE is testing your ability to teach a 'real learner'. Using 'role play' he will be simulating two different learner drivers at different levels of ability, and with differing personalities and characters.

Although you will not be expected to be an expert at using role play yourself, you will need a basic understanding of the subject in order to be able to treat the SE as a real learner.

Role play for training purposes is covered in some detail in section 9.11 and you may find it useful to read that section. It gives guidance to trainers in the use of role play in training.

If an experienced instructor was taking the Part 3, he would be able to draw from his experience gained when teaching many learners with different abilities and personalities. Whatever the SE did on test when playing the part of the pupil, all the instructor would need to do would be to ask himself: 'What would I say and do, if this was a real pupil?'. The answer to this question would probably solve the problem, but you will not have that level of experience to fall back on.

Another problem for you will be that you will not have seen the 'pupil' before. This means that you will be expected quickly to form some idea of the personality and level of knowledge and skill of the person you are teaching.

Skilful use of the Q/A technique will help you to overcome this problem. This is covered in more detail in section 3.2. You will need to ask 'searching' questions, but try not to make your questions sound like an interrogation, as this may alienate the pupil.

Another benefit of asking the 'pupil' questions is that it will help you to settle down into the role of 'instructor'. By the time you have asked your pupil several questions you should be able to relax and treat the SE as you would a real learner. General questions could include:

- How long is it since you had your last lesson?
- Are you able to get any practice in between your lessons?
- Can you remember how many hours driving you have had?

The answers to these questions may then generate other questions.

If the pupil is a novice or partly trained but with very limited experience, you might ask: 'Do you usually drive away from here?'.

If the subject to be taught is one of the manoeuvres, you could ask:

- Have you done any of the other manoeuvres?

- Have you dealt with hill starts or straight reversing?
- Have you learnt 'moving off at an angle'?

By asking this type of question, you may be able to 'link-in' with the lesson to be taught – teaching from the known to the unknown.

If you are dealing with a trained pupil, the questions could include:

- Have you taken a test yet? – and, if failed;
- Have you got your failure sheet with you?

If you receive good training, your trainer should coach you in the use of questions and help you to talk to the SE as if he were a real pupil. The advice given to training establishments in chapter 9 will allow you to measure the effectiveness of the training you are receiving.

If you think that your training is inadequate or ineffective, let your trainer or the principal of the training establishment know of your concern. They have an obligation to give you value for money.

If you have problems in this respect, section 6.1 explains how to be assertive in situations such as these.

SOME COMMON REASONS FOR FAILING

Remember that there are no tricks or traps in the Part 3 examination. Although the SE is playing the part of a pupil, his job is to test your ability to instruct a real pupil.

You should already be familiar with the examiner's marking sheets which are reproduced and covered in detail in *The Driving Instructor's Handbook*. The performance of the PDI is assessed by the SE using a bipolar marking system. At the end of the test, the SE will not advise you whether you have passed or not. The reason for this is that he will have to consider your overall performance before arriving at a decision as to the result. As well as taking into account your performance, he will also take account of his own performance as your 'learner'.

As the marking sheets are quite complex you will be given a copy with your letter advising you of the outcome. You do not really need to understand the way in which the SE arrives at his decision but it is useful to know that serious omissions or errors in fault analysis are regarded as more serious than weaknesses in instructor characteristics.

The main reason that PDIs fail the Part 3 is lack of preparation, or lack of suitable training. This often means that the candidate goes into the examination still finding it difficult to treat the SE as a real learner and consequently losing opportunities to 'bring about learning'. Shortcomings which crop up regularly include the following.

- The inability of the PDI to listen to comments made by his 'pupil' or failure to act on them. For example, if the 'pupil' says, 'Are we going to get any driving done?', it could mean that the PDI is doing too much talking and should perhaps be getting the 'pupil' on the move.
- Inadequate briefing. This is where the PDI does not introduce himself, does not 'set the scene' and asks no questions to establish prior experience.
- Lack of knowledge of the PSTs. This is where the PDI does not cover the subjects that have been asked for, gives explanations which are inadequate, and leaves performance criteria ill-defined.
- Overlong briefings. This can happen when the briefing is not appropriate to the level of understanding or ability of the 'pupil', or where normal briefings are not adjusted to suit the half-hour time span.
- Under-instruction of partly trained 'pupils'. This is where the instructor assumes that the 'pupil' can do things when in fact he may need a talk-through or more prompting to achieve correct driving procedures.
- Over-instruction of trained stage 'pupils'. This could be where the instructor is talking the 'pupil' through situations or over-prompting instead of asking thought provoking questions to encourage the 'pupil' to work out what to do.
- Lack of control of the lesson. This can be where the PDI allows the 'pupil' to keep driving when he should be pulling him over to discuss serious faults; or where the PDI fails to watch how the 'pupil' responds to the instruction given, adjusting the level of instruction accordingly.
- Poor fault assessment, analysis, or correction. This is where the PDI fails to spot faults being made or to deal with them correctly when they are spotted. Sometimes the PDI misses faults other than those connected with the topic being covered on the lesson.
- Failure to correct minor faults on the move.
- Failure to use Q/A technique or act on feedback received.
- Failure to give encouragement when needed and praise when deserved.

If you are in any doubt about any of the above points, you should first of all read the relevant sections in this book covering these aspects of instruction. If you are still in doubt then you should discuss the points with your trainer.

Most of the failure points above can be avoided by using a proper lesson plan. This should include the objectives for the lesson (the MUST KNOW items); how you are going to manage the time available; the method of explaining the main points; any teaching aids which you might need to use. An example of a typical lesson plan is shown on pages 107–8 but remember that the timings are shown as a guide only. The lesson plan will vary depending on the pupil's knowledge, response and receptiveness.

Your trainer should demonstrate to you how the lesson plan needs to be varied to suit specific needs of each 'pupil'.

ON THE DAY OF THE TEST

If you have had sufficient training and are properly prepared for the examination, you should not be feeling too nervous about it. If you do start to feel nervous, take a deep breath and imagine that it is a not the SE sitting next to you, but a 'learner' who knows a lot less than you do!

Make sure you have all your documents and teaching aids with you. You will need:

- your driving licence;
- a certificate of insurance;
- an MOT Certificate if applicable;
- the letter confirming your test appointment;
- L plates or a suitable roof sign incorporating L plates; and
- all your visual aids, any reference books you need and the *Highway Code*.

You will also need to make sure that your car is roadworthy and clean, inside and out. It will also enhance your professional image if you are smartly dressed for the occasion. You may also need:

- a round tray for steering explanation and practice;
- a cloth for cleaning the windows;
- sun glasses if necessary; and
- some mints or a drink.

Do you think that you have had sufficient training to prepare you for the Part 3 examination? Do you fully understand what is required in all the pre-set tests? Will you be able to deal with the SE playing the part of two different learner drivers, with different personalities and levels of understanding and competence? Will you be able to identify faults made, analyse those faults, and offer suitable remedial instruction?

If you can answer 'Yes' to all the above questions you should have a very good chance of passing. You should go into the examination confident that you can deal with any item that the SE presents. This confidence will come from the competence and control that your trainer should have given you.

Keep a clear head and try to be COOL, CALM, COLLECTED, FIRM, FAIR and FRIENDLY.

Remember, keep control. And good luck!

8

The Check Test

This chapter offers advice on how to prepare for the Check Test. Proper use of the Practical Teaching Skills (PTS) in this book should give you greater confidence when taking the Check Test, thus ensuring the best possible grading for your ability.

Unfortunately many instructors see the Check Test as an end in itself. They try to achieve the top grading by 'giving the supervising examiner (SE) what they think he wants to see'.

Tests are of very little value if the information and feedback gained from them is not then fed back into the teaching and learning process.

The basis on which both the check test and the L test are founded is that failure to meet the criteria indicates that the performance is incomplete and needs modifying in some way. The modified performance then needs to be demonstrated again in a further test.

It would be unreasonable to say to one of your pupils who failed the L test 'Well, you had your chance and you blew it!'. Surely, what you would do is book further lessons for that pupil to bring about any improvement necessary, before retaking the test.

Irrespective of the grading you receive, you should be prepared to modify the instruction you are giving so that it takes account of any weaknesses which the test identifies. On the next check test, the SE will be looking to see that any previous recommendations have been implemented.

Some driving instructors find it very difficult to stand back and look at what they are doing in the way that the examiner is able to. They cannot see the wood for the trees! They are often so involved in the teaching that they cannot see whether any learning is taking place.

The check test is useful to instructors in that it provides accessible information that can be used to improve the amount of learning taking place during driving lessons.

> *You should see the check test as being an independent assessment of your teaching ability, the cost of which is included in your registration fee.*

The test is designed so that the examiner can:

ASSESS your teaching ability;
ADVISE you of the outcome and the grading given; and
ASSIST you to make improvements by giving you feedback.

It is natural to be nervous on the test. This, too, is part of your learning process as it will allow you to know first hand what your pupils feel like when they are taking the L test. However, once your natural enthusiasm and the desire to get the best out of your pupil come into play, you should be able to forget the examiner and concentrate instead on giving a normal lesson.

In any examination or test, careful preparation will greatly improve the chances of success. The check test is no different.

You need to know:

1.   What the check test is and why it is carried out;
2.   Who conducts the check test;
3.   When and where the check test will be carried out;
4.   How the check test is conducted;
5.   How to prepare for the check test;

6.   How to present the lesson;
7.   How to get the best grading; and
8.   The result.

8.1

WHAT THE CHECK TEST IS AND WHY IT IS CARRIED OUT

After qualifying as an ADI you have to undergo a check test whenever required to do so by the Registrar.

The statutory requirement is simply an opportunity for the SE to check that your instruction is up to the level required for you to remain on the Register. However, experience has shown that many instructors have misconceptions about what is required. This often makes it difficult for the SE to assess their real ability accurately which results in them receiving an inappropriate grading.

8.2

WHO CONDUCTS THE CHECK TEST

The testing and checking of driving instructors is the responsibility of a relatively small team of supervising examiners who have undertaken extensive specialist training. You and your pupil should be aware that the check test is not related to the L driver testing system. The examiner is there to assess the quality of the instruction being given and not the standard of driving of the pupil.

8.3

WHEN AND WHERE THE CHECK TEST WILL BE CARRIED OUT

If you have recently qualified as an ADI, the SE for your area will soon contact you at your home address to invite you to attend a check test. You will be given a date and time, and the test will start from either the SE's office or from your local driving test centre. If the SE's office is in an area which you are not familiar with, you can elect to take it instead from your local L test centre. You should acknowledge the invitation as soon as possible, letting the SE know immediately if you are unable to attend or if you wish to change the venue.

This first check test is 'educational' in that it is designed to let your local SE, who may not be the one who tested you on the Part 3 exam, see how you perform and let you know if there is anything which needs improving. He will advise you of your grading, provided that it is satisfactory.

If you have been qualified for some time, you will periodically be invited to attend for a check test. The grading you received on your last check test will influence how soon you are requested to undertake a further test.

Again, you should acknowledge the invitation as soon as possible, letting the SE know if you cannot keep the appointment or wish to change the venue. In this case another date and time, or venue, will be offered.

The check test will be conducted during the SE's normal working hours – ie, Mondays to Fridays between 8.30 am and 5.00 pm. If you do not have a pupil available at that time you may give instruction to a full licence holder but this is not advisable. If you do choose to use a full licence holder, you must ensure that the level of instruction is appropriate to their ability. You are not allowed to use another ADI as a pupil.

8.4

HOW THE CHECK TEST IS CONDUCTED

The SE will accompany you while you are giving a driving lesson to a pupil. You are assessed in much the same way as in the ADI examinations but, because the driving lesson is longer than each phase of the Part 3, you must allow more time for the pupil to practice driving.

The SE will be looking for:

• the method, clarity, adequacy and correctness of your instruction;
• your observation and correction of the pupil's errors; and

- your manner, patience and tact in dealing with the pupil, and your ability to inspire confidence.

Remember that the SE is assessing your ability to instruct and not your pupil's ability to drive.

You can give a lesson to a driver at any level of ability – a total novice, an 'experienced' learner or a full licence holder – but the lesson must be tailored to suit the needs of the pupil.

8.5

HOW TO PREPARE FOR THE CHECK TEST

The vehicle in which you conduct your lesson should be safe and reliable, and must carry 'L' plates if you are teaching a pupil who has a provisional licence. If the lesson is conducted in your own or a school car, this should not be a problem. If the lesson is in the pupil's car, it would be sensible to check on the state of the vehicle beforehand. Your ADI certificate must be displayed if you are charging a fee for the lesson.

How you prepare for the lesson should really be no different to what you do for any other lesson. However, you should also be ready to explain to the SE some background information about the pupil and about the lesson you intend to give.

In particular you should let the SE know:

- whether the person is a regular pupil of yours;
- what you know about the pupil's progress;
- what professional instruction they have received;
- whether they are having any private practice;
- any strengths or weaknesses of which you are aware; and
- your lesson plan.

Any teaching aids which you normally use should be prepared in advance. They should be ready and available for use as and when required during the lesson. Notes and any other written material should only be used for reference and should not be read word for word.

8.6

HOW TO PRESENT THE LESSON

The SE wants to see a 'normal' lesson. Do not try to put on a special show for him. Presenting a lesson is covered in full detail in chapter 3, but before the lesson begins you need to take account of the following special requirements.

- Structure the lesson to last about an hour but leave additional time at the end to allow for discussion with the SE.
- Introduce the pupil to the SE and explain the purpose of the visit.
- Emphasise to the pupil that it is you who is being checked.
- Encourage the pupil to behave normally and ask questions if there is anything he does not understand.
- Remind the pupil that because of the extra weight in the back the car may handle slightly differently.

At the beginning of the lesson, depending on the pupil, you may need to confirm with a short recap what was covered in the previous lesson. Asking a couple of questions should tell you whether they have remembered the key points.

Explain to the pupil what is going to be covered in the lesson. This will also let the SE know the objectives of the lesson.

Using your own style, adapt your method of instruction to suit the pupil's ability and personality. The SE will be watching to see that faults do not go uncorrected, that they are corrected in a positive way and that the knowledge that you are passing on is correct.

If the pupil is not one who you teach regularly, make sure that you find out about their previous experience by asking appropriate questions and by inviting the pupil to ask questions.

Although you will have set objectives for the lesson, be prepared to vary your original plan if necessary. For example, if serious problems arise in other areas, concentrate on correcting the more serious items. Give the pupil your reasons for changing the lesson plan and explain that the original topic will be covered in a future lesson.

Your explanations should be methodical and systematic, with a clear definition of the key points of any new subject. Avoid excessive verbalisation or repetition and make sure that the information you give is correct. Encourage the pupil to ask questions if you think that any misunderstanding may have occurred. Your answers should be correct and in sufficient detail for the needs of the individual pupil.

Avoid giving any complicated instructions on the move as this will only distract the pupil and may divert attention away from the driving task. If the pupil asks questions while driving along, answer only briefly, saying 'I want to talk about that when we stop'.

Route directions should be given clearly and in good time. Encourage your pupil to read the road signs and markings. How much guidance you give to them will depend on their ability and experience.

Two very common instructional errors arise from not matching the level of instruction to the ability of the pupil. These are: UNDER-INSTRUCTION and OVER-INSTRUCTION.

UNDER-INSTRUCTION

This often happens when the instructor tries to conduct a mock test letting the pupil drive around and saying nothing until the end. This gives the SE very little information about the method of instruction. Even if the pupil is driving reasonably well, a few mistakes are bound to occur and the instructor can then work on the positive correction of them.

Many experienced instructors feel that if positive correction is given to a pupil at test standard, it will be classed as 'prompting'. However, positive learning is more likely to take place if you draw the pupil's attention to a problem before it gets too serious. Allowing a dangerous situation to develop and then discussing it later is negative or retrospective correction, and is not good teaching practice.

For example, there may be an obstruction on the left and you don't feel that it would be safe to drive through because of approaching traffic. Your pupil, however, is making no attempt to slow down and is obviously heading for the gap. To get the pupil to take some positive action and give way, you could ask, 'Do you think that it is safe to go for that gap? – because I wouldn't want to try it'.

This would be far safer than allowing the pupil to scrape through the gap with unsafe margins for error, then saying 'You shouldn't have gone through that gap – it was dangerous'.

OVER-INSTRUCTION

Unless the pupil is in the very early stages of instruction, or practising a new skill for the first time, try to avoid 'talking them round'. Over-instruction will deter the pupil from thinking and making decisions, which will inhibit progress.

Over-instruction often occurs when the pupil is practising new skills, mixed in with consolidating existing skills. For example, you may be teaching the turn in the road and giving a complete talk-through, but forget that the pupil already knows how to move off and stop. Try to restrict your talk-through to the aspects of the manoeuvre which are new to the pupil.

The question and answer technique may be useful to encourage the pupil to look and plan ahead. It will also tell you what they are thinking. Using the Q/A technique not only tests the pupil's knowledge and understanding, but encourages them to think more about solving problems and making their own decisions. This should also result in a greater degree of participation in the learning task.

For example, if your pupil continually drives too close to parked cars, ask the question 'What will you be looking for approaching these parked cars?'. Or, if bends are being approached at too high a speed, ask 'What will you do if there is an accident just around the bend?'.

OBSERVATION AND PROPER CORRECTION OF ERRORS

Stay alert and try to show an interest in the pupil. Continually look for ways in which to improve their performance. You should recognise all faults and differentiate between those which require immediate attention, and those which are only one-off minor errors.

Constant 'nit-picking' may undermine the confidence of the pupil. Where minor errors occur in isolation, with no effect on safety or control, it may be better not to mention them. This applies particularly in the early stages when the pupil may be under pressure while learning new skills. It can, however, also apply in the later stages of learning. For example, while waiting at a red traffic light with the handbrake on and in neutral, your pupil takes one hand off the wheel to rub his eye.

As the car is secured and the discomfort could cause a distraction, is it really necessary for you to tell him to keep both hands on the wheel?

The causes and consequences of errors should be identified, together with the actions required to prevent recurrence. It is important that corrections are made in a positive manner. For example, 'Drive in the centre of your lane' is much better than 'Don't drive on the white line'. The latter comment only confirms and reinforces what should *not* be done without indicating the correct position on the road.

> *It is no good explaining what the pupil did wrong if you do not explain WHY it is important.*

A good instructor will ask the pupil: 'Why do you think we should keep in the middle of your lane?'.

You should identify and correct the *causes* of any errors and not just the effect of them. For example, if your pupil emerges from a junction without taking effective observation, it should tell you that the potential danger from oncoming traffic has not been understood. Rather than merely confirming the error by saying 'You emerged before you could see properly', it is better to explain the importance of the creep and peep routine.

Whether or not the pupil has understood about limited zones of vision will subsequently be shown by his response in a similar situation. If he demonstrates his ability to use the creep and peep routine, your explanation has obviously been effective. If he still emerges without taking effective observation, he may still not understand the potential danger. A more detailed explanation may be necessary, followed by further practice.

Because of the need for you to be constantly checking all round, it is not always possible to monitor every single mirror check. To avoid any arguments which might arise from undue criticism, rather than stating 'You didn't check your mirrors!', it may be better to ask 'Did you check the mirror before signalling?'.

The response is not really important. What does matter is that the pupil will know whether or not he checked the mirror. Your question will therefore have had the desired effect of making the pupil think about using the mirrors.

MANNER, PATIENCE, TACT AND THE ABILITY TO INSPIRE CONFIDENCE

MANNER – You should try to create a professional but relaxed atmosphere in the car, without becoming over-familiar. How you address your pupils will depend on the background, personality, age and gender of the pupil and yourself. Using first name terms can often lead to a more relaxed atmosphere but in some cases you might need to address your pupil more formally.

Physical contact should be avoided wherever possible as it can be misunderstood and resented. Sit in a position where the pupil cannot accidentally touch you. For example, it could be embarrassing if your leg gets in the way of the handbrake, and the pupil accidentally touches you.

PATIENCE – Just because you may have told the pupil something many times, don't assume that they will necessarily remember it. Be patient! You should be sympathetic and try to rephrase your explanations so that they may be more readily understood. There are different degrees of impatience. These range from sarcastic comments, or tone of voice, and impatient body movements, to total loss of self-control and open hostility towards the pupil.

It will do you no good to get angry in a situation where your pupil already knows that they have done something wrong. Being patient will assist in the learning process by keeping the pupil calm. You will find that this will also lead to a greater degree of co-operation and effort.

TACT – You need to display an awareness of the correct thing to do or say so as to avoid giving offence to a pupil. This requires an intuitive understanding of the needs and feelings of your pupil.

THE ABILITY TO INSPIRE CONFIDENCE – Your own enthusiasm will be reflected in the efforts made by your pupils. They will not normally work as hard if you appear to be bored or disinterested.

Encouragement should be given when needed, and praise should be given where credit is due. This is just as important as the correction of errors, as it will develop the pupil's confidence and inspire further effort.

RECAP – At the end of the lesson you should give your pupil some FEEDBACK on how the lesson has gone, what has been learnt, where possible improvements have taken place and any weak points which will require further instruction.

Look forward to the next lesson, indicating which topics will be covered. Suggest any relevant reading material which needs to be studied in between lessons.

It can be useful to show the SE that you keep records of your pupil's progress and weaknesses. This will show that you are monitoring and assessing what has been covered and what has still to be learnt, and that your pupils are kept informed of their progress.

8.7

HOW TO GET THE BEST GRADING

Preparation for the check test is most important if you wish to get the best possible grading. If you are in doubt over any instructional points you should consider taking some specialist training.

Don't be tempted to use a pupil whose driving is very good – if you select one who needs little or no instruction you will not be able to demonstrate your teaching ability effectively. Using a pupil who has plenty of room for improvement will allow you to bring about some progress during the lesson. This should be one of your prime objectives on the check test.

Make sure that your pupil is properly briefed about the check test – what it is, who will be conducting it and what the procedure will be. Draw up an appropriate lesson plan and make sure that both the pupil and the SE are aware of the objectives for the lesson. Don't try to cram too many things into the one lesson. It is better to bring about some improvement in one aspect of driving than try to improve the overall ability of the pupil in all aspects.

Your instruction should be based on the lesson plan and the pupil's ability but be prepared to modify the objectives if necessary. Flexibility is the key to good instruction.

Brief your pupils at the start of the lesson, give feedback during the lesson if appropriate and make time to give a thorough debriefing and some feedback at the end. Involve your pupils as much as possible by using the Q/A technique and inviting questions from them.

Try to avoid too much retrospective instruction. Be positive and identify any faults made, analysing their causes. Think about and discuss solutions, getting your pupil to work with you in improving any weak points.

SELF-ASSESSMENT BEFORE THE CHECK TEST

In assessing your overall instructional ability, the SE will in particular be considering your:

- individual characteristics as an instructor;
- instruction/teaching ability; and
- fault identification, analysis, and correction.

Before you take the check test analyse your own performance in these three areas.

Instructor characteristics

Clarity – Are your verbal instructions clear and articulate?

Enthusiasm – Do you sound enthusiastic about the subject and the progress the pupil is making?

Encouragement – Do you encourage the pupil as often as you should?

Manner – Are you friendly and able to put your pupil at ease?

Patience and tact – Do you sound impatient or show your impatience or lack of tact when the pupil gets something wrong?

Instructional techniques

Recap at the start of the lesson – Do you remind the pupil what was covered and achieved in the previous lesson?

Objectives – Do you clearly define and state the objectives for the lesson you are giving?

Level of instruction – Do you match the level of instruction to suit the needs and ability of each pupil?

Instructions given – Are they easy for the pupil to understood or are they sometimes ambiguous?

Language – Do you keep it simple, avoiding jargon and technical words that the pupil may not understand?

Q/A technique – Do you use questions effectively and invite questions from your pupil?

Feedback – Do you give it yourself and gain it from your pupil and, if so, do you act properly on it?

Recap at the end of the lesson – Does your pupil get out of the car knowing what has been achieved and feeling good?

Use of dual controls – Do you use the dual controls only when necessary or do you use them excessively?

Fault assessment

Fault identification – Do you always accurately identify faults made by your pupils?

Fault analysis – Do you analyse the faults made in such a way that you pupil understands what has gone wrong and how to put it right?

Remedial action – Do you make sure that your pupils have the opportunity to remedy any faults made?

Timing of fault – Do you assess faults made while they are still fresh in the pupil's mind, or do you leave it so late that your pupil cannot recall the situation?

If you are in any doubt about any of these check points, you should refer to earlier chapters in this book which cover them in more detail.

SOME DO'S AND DON'TS

DO

- Prepare in advance – your car, the pupil, the lesson plan.
- Take account of any recommendations the SE may have made in any previous check test.
- Brief both the pupil and the SE.
- Pitch the instruction at an appropriate level.
- Use a two-way Question and Answer technique.
- Ensure that some learning takes place during the lesson.
- Identify, analyse and correct any faults.
- Use encouragement when needed, and praise when deserved.
- Sum up at the end of the lesson and look forward to the next one.

DON'T

- Choose a pupil for their good driving ability.
- Use too much retrospective instruction.
- Involve the SE in the lesson.
- Try to carry out a mock test.

You owe it to yourself to obtain the best possible grading. If you are at all worried about the standard of your instruction, then consider taking some specialist training to prepare you for the check test.

8.8

THE RESULT

At the end of the check test the SE will have ASSESSED your instruction. He will then ADVISE you of the result out of earshot of your pupil. He will discuss your performance with you and ASSIST you in bringing about any improvement necessary.

If you have passed, you will be given a grade – 4, 5 or 6. If you are given a grade 4 this means that your instruction was only adequate. A grade 5 means that your instruction was good; a grade 6 indicates that the instruction observed was very good indeed.

At this stage you will be given the opportunity to discuss with the SE anything that you do not understand about the grading given or any recommendations that are made. These recommendations are designed to help you to build on your strengths and correct any weak points.

The grade awarded will determine how soon you will be asked to take the next check test. As a rough guide, you could normally expect to be seen again within two years if you achieved a grade 4, three years if you achieved a grade 5, or four years if you achieved a grade 6.

If you have failed, the SE will tell you how soon you will be required to retake the test. Any grade below 4 will require a further check test fairly soon. If you got a grade 3 you will normally be seen within three months; with a grade 2 you will be seen again within two months. In each case, the SE will expect to see a significant improvement on the next check test. You should seriously consider taking retraining to bring your instruction up to the required standard.

If there is anything the SE has explained that you don't fully understand, the chances are you will find more detail about it in this book. Use the contents pages and the index to find the appropriate section.

Failing that, you can always telephone the SE in his office on a Friday if you have any difficulty in understanding or implementing his recommendations.

If you fail a further check test with an SE, you will then be required to take another test with a more senior examiner. At this stage if your instruction has not improved the Registrar will consider removing your name from the Register of ADIs.

Should you be given a grade 1 on your initial check test, this would indicate that your instruction is considered to be dangerous. In this case, a second test will be arranged very quickly. If your instruction is still considered dangerous, you would not normally be allowed a third attempt.

In all cases of failure, the examiner will confirm in writing what aspects of instruction were considered inadequate or wrong.

Irrespective of any recommendations that your SE makes, you should always ask yourself:

- Was there anything more I could have done to make my teaching more effective so as to bring about more learning for my pupil?
- How can I go about implementing the suggestions made by the SE?

Finally, GOOD LUCK when you next take your check test!

9

Driving Instructor Training

The fact that the pass rate for the ADI Part 3 examination is only 30 per cent gives an indication of the need for guidance for training establishments and trainers, particularly those preparing candidates for this part of the examination.

Earlier in this book we have covered in detail the preparation for all three parts of the ADI examinations, information which will be of interest to trainers and trainees. In this chapter we deal with the registration procedures for the ADITE and DIARTE schemes and the advantages to be gained in becoming 'Approved' by those running training establishments.

This knowledge should be beneficial to proprietors of training establishments, those providing the training and PDIs who may be seeking training.

9.1

APPROVED TRAINING ESTABLISHMENTS

An Approved Training Establishment is one which has undergone inspection by specially qualified DSA SEs/ADI (inspectors) and has attained the minimum standards required for approval under the two schemes.

A common objective of the ADITE and DIARTE schemes is to administer a Directory of Approved Driving Instructor Training Establishments in order to:

a)   Establish and maintain minimum standards of driving instructor training for those establishments on the list.
b)   Assist members of the public wishing to undergo training to become ADIs, and existing ADIs wishing to undergo retraining, through the provision of minimum standards for Approved Training Establishments.
c)   Contribute more positively towards an improvement in standards of road safety in Great Britain.

9.2

THE ADITE AND DIARTE SCHEMES

The idea to have an industry-run register of driving instructor training establishments was initiated by the Approved Driving Instructors National Joint Council (ADI/NJC). It had long been felt that there was a need for the industry to present a more collective and professional presence in the training being offered to prospective driving instructors and the retraining of existing ADIs.

In April 1988 a joint working party (JWP) was established, with representatives from all the ADI groups with consultative status, together with representatives of the DSA. After consultation with the Training Agency it was agreed that the group should be widened to include the British School of Motoring, which is the biggest ADI training provider in the country. The BSM was consequently invited to join the JWP and thereafter took part.

The JWP, which at that time included the DIA, presented its final report in February 1991 and received immediate Ministerial support. The DIA made a unilateral decision to create its own register of approved training establishments.

The remaining members of the JWP formed a company limited by guarantee on 23 March 1992 to administer the Directory of Approved Driving Instructor Training Establishments, known as ADITE. Currently, the directors of the company comprise one member from each of the following ADI organisations which have Driving Standards Agency consultative status:

The Approved Driving Instructors' National Joint Council (ADI/NJC)
The British School of Motoring Limited (BSM)
The Motor Schools' Association of Great Britain Limited (MSA)

Within ADITE the positions of Chairman, Secretary and Treasurer are filled on an annual rotating basis by a nominated representative from each of the member organisations.

Approved Driving Instructor Training Establishments

The directors of ADITE act as a management committee, with a permanent Secretary administering the day-to-day running of the Directory.

As the task of improving standards is an ongoing one, a Standards Committee has been formed, with one representative from each of the three consultative organisations together with an equal number of representatives who are elected annually by, and drawn from, those on the ADITE directory.

To gain entry to the ADITE directory, establishments are inspected by specially trained Supervising Examiners (SEs/ADI), with a re-inspection every two years. Inspections cover:

PREMISES – These must be suitable and conform to the requirements of the Health and Safety at Work Act and any other statutory legislation appropriate to the number of trainees.
VEHICLES – These must be suitable for the purpose and conform to all relevant statutory requirements.

TRAINING – This must ensure that the needs of each trainee are individually assessed, and that the tuition given is structured so as to cover all the topics required for ADI registration.

There must be continuous assessment of each trainee's progress, with no major errors or omissions in the subject matter or the manner in which it is being taught.

CODE OF PRACTICE – This must be displayed at the training establishment, given to each course participant and strictly adhered to.

ADMINISTRATION – Full records of each person trained must be properly maintained.

Further details of the ADITE directory can be obtained from:

> ADITE
> PO Box 101
> Stockport
> Cheshire
> SK4 4DW

Driving Instructors Association Recommended Training Establishments

The directors of DIA International Limited have formed their own recommended list of training establishments – The Driving Instructors Association Register of Training Establishments (DIARTE).

The aims of DIARTE are similar to those of ADITE with inspections being carried out by DSA SEs/ADI to the same criteria as ADITE.

Further details of the DIARTE scheme can be obtained by writing to:

> DIARTE
> Safety House
> Beddington Farm Road
> Croydon
> Surrey
> CR0 4XZ

9.3

CODE OF PRACTICE

To maintain acceptable minimum standards, those seeking approval under the schemes must abide by the CODE OF PRACTICE shown below.

Code of Practice

Those who train or retrain Driving Instructors must:

a)   Clearly inform all prospective customers in writing, details of the services being offered including venue, duration, cost and content.

b)   Ensure that training takes account of individual student needs within the framework of the course.

c)   Apply an honest, moral and professional approach in all business practice.

d)   Have a complaints procedure

e)   Take all reasonable care and skill to ensure the safety of students.

f)   Ensure that all vehicles and equipment used in training are maintained in a safe and satisfactory condition.

g)   Comply with the current legislation in particular with regard to the following:
   i   business premises and practice;
   ii   staff;
   iii   vehicles;
   iv   public liability.

This Code of Practice must be clearly displayed at the Training Establishment and a copy must be given to each course participant.

Facilities

The level of facilities available at any time should be commensurate with the total number of students on each course and include:

a)   Training Plan

b)   Course curriculum

c)   Resource material
d)   Training aids
e)   A suitable motor car/cars
f)   The availability of: 1) a classroom; 2) toilet and washroom;
      3) refreshments; 4) classroom teaching aids (OHP etc)

9.4

TRAINERS

Those engaged in training or retraining driving instructors for an
Establishment must be suitable persons who are able to:

a)   Impart an understanding of the role of the ADI in teaching
      pupils the skills required to drive Motor Cars safely.
b)   Teach students lifetime attitudes and skills that make
      proficient, responsible instructors.
c)   Communicate effectively orally and in writing.
d)   Teach the student the theoretical and practical requirements
      for the ADI Register examination and current regulations.
e)   Teach effectively in a classroom and in an in-car environment
      as applicable.
f)   Construct a flexible training programme to take account of the
      needs of students within the framework of the course.
g)   Indicate sources of further training.
h)   Advise students of the role of Road Safety and ADI
      organisations.
i)   Assess the individual needs of the student and offer adequate
      guidance in business management.
j)   Advise students as to the conditions applicable to equal opportunities.

9.5

ADITE AND DIARTE INSPECTION PROCEDURES

a)   A need exists to inspect Training Establishments to establish
      and maintain minimum standards of Driving Instructor
      Training and retraining for Approved Training Establishments.

b)   There will be an initial inspection up to six months before the establishment becomes Approved followed by further inspections every two years thereafter.

c)   The inspecting officers will be DSA SEs/ADI especially trained and selected for the task, and will not normally be the same SE/ADI who conducts tests of continued ability and fitness to give instruction in the establishment's area.

d)   A facility will be available for interim inspection on request.

e)   Inspections will take place at a venue agreed between the inspector and the Principal of the training establishment.

f)   It is in the interests of the Principal of the training establishment to provide a venue which is compatible with the type of training to be inspected and will allow the inspector to assess all the facilities.

g)   The inspecting officer will visit the establishment by appointment and will observe both the facilities available and the training taking place.

h)   An assessment will be made with the observations being recorded on a reporting document and a copy given to the Principal.

i)   A discussion will take place during which the Inspecting Officer will advise the Principal of any possible improvements or changes which may be required.

j)   Within 14 days the Principal will receive a written report from the Inspecting Officer and a copy will be forwarded to either the ADITE Management Committee or to DIARTE.

9.6

APPLICATIONS

Application forms for registration can be obtained from ADITE or DIARTE. The completed application form for registration should be sent with the registration fee to ADITE or DIARTE. On receipt of this, ADITE or DIARTE will arrange for the DSA to send the training establishment an application form for inspection.

The inspection form includes notes for guidance and the current scale of inspection fees. When completed, this should be sent with the appropriate inspection fee direct to:

> Driving Standards Agency
> Stanley House
> 56 Talbot Road
> Nottingham   NG1 5GU
>
> *Telephone* 0115 955 7600

9.7

INSPECTION DOCUMENTATION AND ASSESSMENT SHEETS

It will be of help to training establishments considering inspections with a view to becoming Approved to understand how the establishment is assessed during the inspection.

The following assessment forms are used which incorporate a bipolar marking system similar to that used on the ADI Check Test.

At the end of the inspection, the Inspecting Officer will refer to his assessment sheets (shown following) and will take an overview of the inspection carried out, drawing up report sheets giving:

- an overview of the facilities seen;
- a report on individual trainers' performance;
- an overview of all training;
- a summary of the visit;
- any recommendations; and
- general comments.

The following marking sheets will be used by the Inspecting Officer. It is pointed out that, although at the time of going to press these marking sheets are current, they are under continuous review.

DRIVING STANDARDS AGENCY
ASSESSMENT REPORT

T/E No_____

ESTABLISHMENT NAME_____

PRINCIPALS NAME   _____

LOCATION OF VISIT _____

_____POST CODE _____

TELEPHONE CONTACT POINT _____

NUMBER OF TRAINERS AT THIS ESTABLISHMENT _____

NUMBER OF TRAINERS SEEN ON THIS VISIT   _____

NAMES OF TRAINERS SEEN

_____   _____

_____   _____

_____   _____

NAMES OF TRAINERS EMPLOYED

_____   _____

_____   _____

_____   _____

_____   _____

DATE _____ NO OF DAYS ON INSPECTION _____

INSPECTOR _____ SECTION NO_____

SIGNED_____DATE_____

form TE/03

Assessment report form TE/03

DRIVING STANDARDS AGENCY
ASSESSMENT REPORT

TE. Ref No.

FACILITIES: UNACCEPTABLE   to   VERY GOOD

a.   Training Plan

b.   Course Curricula

c.   Resource Material

d.   Training Aids

e.   Motor Vehicle/s

f. Standards and Availability of:

    i.   Classroom

    ii. Toilet/
        Cloakroom

    iii. Refreshments

    iv. Classroom Aids
        (OHP etc)

Notes.

Form TE/03a

Assessment form TE/03a

**DRIVING STANDARDS AGENCY
ASSESSMENT REPORT**

INSTRUCTION OBSERVED DURING VISIT

SUBJECTS COVERED   UNACCEPTABLE   to   VERY GOOD

....

....

....

....

....

....

TRAINEE'S RESPONSE TO TRAINING

POOR   to   VERY GOOD

....

....

....

....

....

....

form TE/03b

Assessment form TE/03b

DRIVING STANDARDS AGENCY
ASSESSMENT REPORT

NAME OF TRAINER..

SUBJECT..

TRAINER CHARACTERISTICS

Inarticulate							Articulate

Indifferent							Enthusiastic

Discouraging							Encouraging

Aloof							Friendly

Impatient							Patient

Lacking Confidence							Confident

TRAINING TECHNIQUES

Objectives Unclear							Clear

Level of Instruction Unsuitable							Suitable

Instructions Ambiguous							Easily U'stood

Language Over Technical							Simple

Q/A Techniques Ineffective							Effective

Feedback Not Given							Given

Recap at Start None							Thorough

Recap at End None							Thorough

NOTES

form TE/03c

Assessment form TE/03c

DRIVING STANDARDS AGENCY
ASSESSMENT REPORT

<u>FAULT ASSESSMENT</u>

Faults Not Identified							Identified
Fault Analysis Not Attempted							Offered
Fault Analysis Incorrect							Correct
Remedial Action Not Offered							Suggested
Fault Assessment Unnecessarily Late							At Correct Time

<u>ROLE PLAY/FAULT SIMULATION</u>

		1	2	3	4	5	6	
DIRECTIONS ON ROUTE	POOR							GOOD
CONTROL OF LESSON	POOR							GOOD
PUPILS QUERIES	POOR							GOOD
SETTING THE SCENE	POOR							CORRECT
PLAYING THE ROLE	UNDER							CORRECT
PLAYING THE ROLE	OVER							CORRECT
MAINTAINING THE ROLE	POOR							GOOD
FAULTS	TOO FEW							CORRECT
FAULTS	TOO MANY							CORRECT
OVERALL CONTENT	UNREALISTIC							REALISTIC
ASSESSMENTS	INCORRECT							CORRECT

<u>NOTES</u>

form TE/03d

Assessment form TE/03d

9.8

GENERAL GUIDANCE IN PREPARING FOR THE INSPECTION

Before the inspection day go through the criteria and standards detailed in this chapter and make sure that you are complying with all the requirements for Approval.

When the Inspecting Officer arrives at the training establishment it is advisable that the Principal finds time to explain to him the background of the trainee/s, details of the trainers to be seen and what subjects are to be covered. Any other information which will assist the Inspecting Officer in carrying out the assessment should be volunteered – for example, course syllabus, any relevant course material etc.

Make sure that the Inspecting Officer knows exactly what he is inspecting and that all parties involved are on the same wavelength.

Wherever possible preparation for all three parts of the ADI qualifying examinations should be demonstrated but, if this is not possible, the emphasis should be placed on the practical element.

Classroom skills could be demonstrated by briefing the trainees on what is to be covered during the practical sessions to follow.

If preparation for Part 2 (own driving) is to be demonstrated, do not merely assess the driving skills of the trainee/s. Make sure that practical instruction is given in improving their driving ability.

When preparing candidates for the Part 3, many trainers fail to recognise the problems of PDIs who have little or no experience of teaching real learners. For example, an experienced ADI should find it relatively simple to switch the level of instruction from one pupil to another.

The PDI is expected on the test to be able to teach a 'pupil' at one level of ability, with whatever personality or character the SE has decided to adopt, for 28 minutes. Then, immediately after, and under pressure, he has to begin teaching a pupil with a different personality and character, at a different level of ability.

While the PDIs may make a good job of covering whatever subjects have been chosen, it is often the inability to deal with the 'pupil', and the lack of flexibility and adaptability, that causes them to fail.

The trainer must therefore spend some time on this aspect of training. It is not enough for the PDI to learn the pre-set tests, although this might be seen as a starting point. The PDI should have a basic understanding of how to match the level of instruction to the level of ability of the 'pupil' and also how to deal with pupils with different personality traits. If the trainer was taking the Part 3 in any given situation, all he would need to do is ask himself 'What would I say and what would I do if this was a real pupil?'. If the PDI has never taught a real pupil, how can he be expected to ask that question?

Trainers should, therefore, go out of their way to give the PDIs practical experience of dealing with pupils with differing personalities and levels of ability. Later in this chapter we will be dealing specifically with role play, including the five different role modes adopted by the SE on the Part 3 test.

9.9

AFTER THE INSPECTION

The completed inspection report is submitted to the DSA where it is considered by a senior examiner (currently an Assistant Chief Driving Examiner). He will then refer the report back to either the ADITE management committee or DIARTE with a recommendation for Approval or rejection. The ADITE management committee or DIARTE will then decide whether Approval should be granted.

Training establishments will be notified of the outcome as soon as possible after the decision has been reached.

Unsuccessful applicants will be notified in detail of the reasons why Approval has not been given and invited to apply again once any shortcomings have been remedied.

At the end of the inspection when the Inspecting Officer gives you the debriefing of what he has seen, let him know if there has been any misunderstanding. Remember he is there to help you to improve your performance and you would do well to listen to any advice given. If any specific recommendations are made, try to take account of them in future training sessions.

If you and your trainers make good use of the practical teaching skills covered in this book, you should have no problem in satisfying the Inspecting Officer that your trainees have benefited from the training you have provided.

Chapter 7 in this book will be of great interest to those training PDIs for all three parts of the ADI qualifying examinations. *The Driving Instructor's Handbook* (Kogan Page) will also be useful as a reference manual, particularly for those preparing candidates for the Part 1 (Written) examination.

Irrespective of any advice given by the Inspecting SE, at the end of each training session, your trainers should ask themselves: 'Has learning taken place? Is there anything more I could have done for my trainees to assist them in the learning process?'.

On completion of a formal training course, the course trainers should be prepared to recommend further training for those trainees who require it.

Maintaining accurate records is one of the requirements of Approval. Apart from the Inspection Report you should monitor the progress of your trainees and keep records of their examination results. This will give you some indication as to how successful the training you have given has been.

Proprietors should consider devising a 'course evaluation question-naire' to be completed by course participants at the end of a training course with a view to gaining feedback. The objective of this is to identify areas where improvements can be made.

A sample questionnaire is shown below:

INSTRUCTOR TRAINING CENTRE   COURSE EVALUATION QUESTIONNAIRE

Please complete the following questionnaire to enable us to consider ways of improving the course that you have taken.

You do not need to put your name on the questionnaire and please feel free to comment on anything that you were unhappy with or feel is relevant.

We wish you to evaluate three areas:- PREMISES (Classroom, restroom, toilet, refreshments etc.), VEHICLE (Any training vehicle used on the course), TRAINING RECEIVED (The course content and the way in which it was presented).

PLEASE TICK THE APPROPRIATE BOX UNDER EACH OF THE THREE HEADINGS

	PREMISES	VEHICLE	TRAINING PROVIDED
Better than expected?	[ ]	[ ]	[ ]
As you expected?	[ ]	[ ]	[ ]
Not as good as expected?	[ ]	[ ]	[ ]

Do you think you have received good value for money?   YES/NO

Is there anything different you would have liked to have seen on the course?

Any other comments about the course or the trainer/s please write below or overleaf. Thank you for your assistance.

9.10

QUALIFICATIONS FOR TRAINERS

In the absence of any National Vocational Qualification (NVQ) or any other nationally recognised qualification within the industry, the JWP were not able to recommend any single qualification for ADI trainers. It was agreed, however, that there are a number of qualifications which would be useful to those providing ADI training.

If the trainers are not well qualified, you could have a situation where a training establishment has excellent facilities and course curriculum, but the training provided is of poor quality. The customer would not, in this case, be getting value for money.

It was agreed that the following qualifications would be useful for ADI trainers:

- The AEB/DIA Diploma in driving instruction. (This would give a good foundation of knowledge for any driving instructor wishing to train instructors.)
- The Cardington Special Driving Test (Grade A Pass). (This would be particularly relevant for those involved in preparing candidates for the Part 2.)
- The City & Guilds 7307 Further and Adult Education Teaching Certificate. (This would be particularly useful for those engaged in any form of classroom teaching.)
- The City & Guilds 7254 Certificate in Training Competence. (This would be most appropriate for those preparing candidates for the Parts 2 and 3.)
- The ADI National Joint Council Tutors Certificate. (This would give a good foundation for those who train or retrain driving instructors.)
- The Motor Schools Association Tutors Certificate. (This would give a good foundation for those who train or retrain driving instructors.)

Since the work of the JWP ceased with the formation of ADITE there are several new qualifications for trainers which are based on national standards produced by the Training and Development Lead Body, which includes full NVQs in Training and Development.

These new qualifications not only provide individuals with national recognition of their competence, but also give training organisations the opportunity to assess and accredit their own 'in-house' training programmes.

The new qualifications are:

* City & Guilds NVQ Level 3 in Training & Development (7291/01);
* City & Guilds NVQ Level 4 in Training & Development (7281/02);
* City & Guilds NVQ Level 4 in Training & Development (Design and Delivery) (7281/03).

As part of the assessment process, candidates for the above awards are encouraged to present a portfolio identifying prior achievements which can provide credit towards an award. This could include evidence which is considered appropriate, including reports, endorsements from employers and training notes. Qualifications already held by trainers which can also be used as part of this portfolio, include the City & Guilds 725 Direct Trainer's Certificate, The City & Guilds 730 Further and Adult Education Teacher's Certificate, The City & Guilds 7254 Certificate in Training Competence, The City & Guilds 7255 Direct Trainer's Certificate and any other relevant teaching qualification.

To give some guidance to training establishments and trainers who may be considering NVQs, the Training and Development Lead Body has identified four phases of activity which must be represented in any NVQ, shown in the training cycle below:

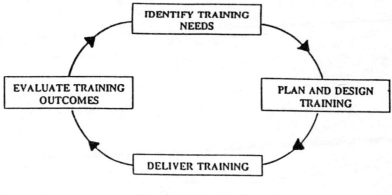

The Training Cycle

9.11

ROLE-PLAY SKILLS

When preparing trainees for the instructional ability examination, the most common weakness of trainers is often the poor use of role play skills. Trainers who are weak in their own use of role play and their ability to teach role play to their trainees should consider seeking specialist training themselves.

What is role play?

A role-play used for training purposes is a simulation in which trainers and/or trainees are required to act out the role of an individual in a situation or circumstances that are relevant to the trainee. The scenario could be an imaginary one or a real situation that the trainee is likely to face in the future. In practice, most role-plays take the form of a short, unscripted playlet involving two or more participants taking the parts of different people.

Why use role play?

Role playing is a valuable technique for the trainer. It can provide participation, involvement and the opportunity for action learning. Participants can practise dealing with situations which could occur in real life in a protected environment.

Their communication skills, behaviour and feelings during the exercise can form the basis for self-appraisal and feedback from the trainer. From this, trainees will learn which words, behaviour and approaches are effective. Mistakes can be made and learnt from in a risk-free way. Apart from on the check test, this opportunity to receive feedback rarely, if ever, occurs once they are back at work doing their job.

Role playing can provide a mirror for participants to see themselves as others see them. This encourages insight into their own behaviour and sensitivity to others' opinions, attitudes and needs. The benefits of changes in behaviour or attitude can readily be demonstrated, thus bringing about any desired modification.

The effectiveness of role playing as a training tool is dependent on the quality of the feedback and the control of the trainer. Feedback must be constructive or it becomes counter-productive, saps confidence and erects barriers to learning. Positive feedback can reinforce effective behaviour, instil confidence and highlight specific areas for improvement in a way that is readily accepted by the trainee.

Designing role-play exercises in the training function

The design of the exercise should be governed by the need for the role play to contribute to the overall training objectives. Three factors need to be considered:

CREDIBILITY – The degree to which the situation is identifiable by the trainee.

RELEVANCE – The scenario must allow the trainer to extract the learning points required from the situation to be played.

COMPLEXITY – The level of complexity must reflect the knowledge, understanding and ability of the trainee.

CONTROL OF THE EXERCISE

To get the best out of the role-play exercise, the trainer must maintain overall control in an activity where it is difficult to predict what is going to happen. The trainer must be ready to intervene if things take off in ways that are not going to be helpful to the trainee or where danger is involved.

In order for the trainer to guide the role-play exercise, he needs to be: 1) PROACTIVE, and 2) REACTIVE.

Proactive mode

Having gone into the role of the character to be played, in the proactive mode the trainer is likely to ask questions of the trainee to test knowledge, understanding, attitude and ability. He will take opportunities as the session develops to prompt response and test the trainee's flexibility.

Reactive mode

Acting on the level of ability and character of the person being portrayed, the trainer will do exactly as he is told. He will respond well to any instruction given, following instructions to the letter but with safety in mind.

When planning their role-play exercises in training, it will be useful for trainers to understand how the SE uses role play for testing purposes in the Part 3 exam.

SEs' USE OF ROLE PLAY IN THE PART 3

Many PDIs fail the exam because they have had inadequate practical experience of teaching pupils, either real or simulated. Unless they are very well prepared, they tend to 'read what's on the label and accept what is says, rather than look to see what's in the bottle'. This often means that on the Part 3 they do not know how to react to an SE who is either being PROACTIVE or REACTIVE and will be playing one of five different role modes. These are:

> NEGATIVE;
> SIMPLE;
> AVERAGE;
> TESTING; and
> KNOWLEDGEABLE.

At the start of the Part 3 the SE should be clear in his own mind whether he is to be PROACTIVE or REACTIVE. He will normally start by being proactive in each of the two phases. This makes it easier to decide what faults to display and they way in which they are to be made. He will then respond to instruction given in a reactive way.

Proactive

The SE decides the level of ability of the pupil to be portrayed and remains within the role if the PDI does not attempt to correct the faults. He is likely to ask questions of the 'instructor' to prompt response and will take opportunities, as they develop on the drive, to test the PDI's flexibility.

Reactive

The SE, acting on the level of ability to be portrayed, responds to instruction given by the PDI whether correct, incorrect or late. Unless there is danger to the SE, or other road users, the SE should always respond to the PDI's instruction as given, and assess it accordingly.

It will be useful for trainers when role-playing to understand just how the SE puts this into practice. When preparing for the role-play exercise, the trainer should consider the 'role mode' of the character, ie:

PROACTIVE MODE
1. NEGATIVE – Waits for the PDI to use Q/A to establish knowledge and understanding. Responds 'Yes' when asked if he understands the question.
2. SIMPLE – Does not respond to technical instruction waiting for the PDI to adjust level of instruction to suit the pupil.
3. AVERAGE – Asks questions in a normal, sensible way relevant to the subject being taught.
4. TESTING – Pupil's questions go beyond what is being taught. (eg, 'What if . . .?'). Waits for PDI to deal positively with this.
5. KNOWLEDGEABLE (knows it all) – Challenges instruction being given. Picks up incorrect instruction by saying 'Why do I need to do that then?' etc.

REACTIVE MODE
1. NEGATIVE – Responds normally to PDI's use of Q/A. Can ask further questions to clarify.
2. SIMPLE – Once PDI adjusts level of instruction to suit pupil, SE queries technical matters.
3. AVERAGE – Follows instruction given, right or wrong, unless it is not safe to do so.
4. TESTING – When PDI reacts and takes control, SE keeps to the subject in hand but is ready for 'What ifs . . .?' on new subjects.
5. KNOWLEDGEABLE – When PDI takes control the SE offers less challenges to the instruction being given. Picks up incorrect instruction by saying 'That's not what my last instructor said' etc.

The SE can use the above role modes and character traits in any way that he feels appropriate, but should not be using the same two combinations in any Part 3 examination and will rarely choose to be the 'average' pupil. In order to adequately prepare PDIs to be able to deal with the SE playing the role of two different 'learners', trainers should role play different types of drivers, at different levels of ability, committing a range of driver errors. The level of ability and the stage of training of the PDI should also be taken into account. This will prevent PDIs from feeling threatened by being asked to deal with pupils they are not yet ready to cope with. To overcome this problem, when carrying out role-play exercises the trainer should follow suitable performance criteria and range statements.

Suitable performance criteria would be:

a) The role adopted and faults simulated are realistic and typical of the driver being portrayed.

b) The role and errors are appropriate to the learning topic outlined at the commencement of the exercise.

c) A suitable briefing is given to the PDI, outlining the objectives of the exercise and the topic being covered.

d) The role adopted and errors simulated are at a level of complexity relevant to the needs and ability of the trainee.

e) It is always clear to the trainee when the trainer is in role or out of it.

f) Driver error simulation never causes safety to be sacrificed.

g) The role adopted and driver errors simulated never undermine the confidence of the PDI.

h) Detailed verbal feedback is provided. (This should include accurate measurement and analysis of performance, degree of competence achieved and any remedial action which needs to be taken.)

i) Detailed written feedback is provided.

Range statements should cover:

a) Type of role, from simple to complex person.

b) Type of role, from proactive to reactive.

c) Type of driver error simulated, from rote-type to poor observation, poor forward planning, poor risk assessment and making incorrect decisions.

d) Type of driving ability, from novice, partly trained, trained.

When playing the role of the pupil, the trainer should bear in mind that he has to give any directions to the PDI in time for them to be relayed back.

The use of video during role play exercises can be a valuable aid in assessing performance and during feedback sessions. The use of in-car video would be useful but is difficult to implement.

Effective debriefing and feedback after any in-car role-play exercises are therefore essential.

In any role-play exercise, the trainer should:

- fully brief the participants before the exercise on the topic being covered and its objectives;
- ensure that the role/s being adopted are relevant to the topic being covered and its objectives;
- always make it clear to the trainee when the trainer is in role or out of it;
- never undermine the confidence of the trainee; and
- provide detailed written feedback to help the trainee to reflect on his performance.

9.12

THE IMPORTANCE OF GAINING FEEDBACK FROM TRAINEES

An example of feedback in a closed system is the automatic switch controlling the electric fan which helps to cool your radiator. When the water in the radiator starts to get too hot, it feeds back information about the temperature which starts the fan. When the radiator cools down, the fan stops. As the driver you don't have to do anything about it. It is automatic.

In training, nothing is automatic. It is not a closed system. It is dynamic and changes with time and experience. Feedback in learning or training requires not only some way of monitoring change from inside but also input from outside.

We need a mirror to show us an image of what we are doing, or what we are not; some means of judging how effective our training is.

When we work with people, they provide that mirror for us if we take the trouble to use it. Just as we use the mirrors on our car, looking is not enough. We need to know what we are looking for, how to assess what we see and how we are going to act on what is seen.

In section 3.2 we have covered the importance of giving and gaining feedback. Those who train driving instructors will find that gaining feedback from PDIs who have taken the ADI entrance examinations will be most useful.

Irrespective of whether the candidate has passed or failed, the feedback gained will help the trainer to identify any weaknesses in the training provided.

Immediate communication by telephone after the test is desirable, but where this is not possible, questionnaires could be devised for all three parts of the examination, requesting feedback from the candidate on how the examination went.

Examples are shown below:

WRITTEN EXAMINATION QUESTIONNAIRE

Name of candidate..   Tel:......................

What date did you take the examination?...................

Did you pass or fail?...................   Was it your 1st attempt..............

If not, what attempt was it?.........   What mark did you get?..........

Do you think that your resource material covered
all the questions you were asked?   ....Y/N

Do you think that you did enough studying for the
examination before taking it?   ....Y/N

Did you do a) as well as expected or b) better
than expected   [Put a) or b)] ....

Please write below any questions you can remember which you did not know or understand.

....

....

....

Continue overleaf if necessary.
Thank you for your co-operation. We will be in touch.

PART 2 (Own driving) EXAMINATION QUESTIONNAIRE

Name of candidate... Tel...........................

Date of test.............................. Place....................................

Did you pass or fail?................... Which attempt was it?..............
If you passed, did the SE have any comments to make about your driving? If so please give details below.

....

If you failed, what did you fail on? Please give details below.

....

Was there anything that happened during the drive about which you were uncertain? If so, please give details overleaf.

Thank you for your co-operation. We will be in touch.

PART 3 PRACTICAL EXAMINATION QUESTIONNAIRE

Name of candidate... Tel....................
Date of test.............................. Place....................................

Did you pass or fail?................. Which attempt was it?..............

What subjects were you asked to cover in the Pre-set test given?

Phase 1   ....

Phase 2   ....

What grading did you get on Phase 1.................Phase 2...................

Do you feel that these gradings accurately reflect your performance?

(Y/N) Phase 1............................ Phase 2.............................

Was there anything that happened during either phase about which you were uncertain? Please give details overleaf.

Do you feel that you were adequately prepared for the test?.......Y/N

If not, why not? ....

Thank you for your co-operation. We will be in touch.

By studying the questionnaires, the training establishment/trainer will be able to identify any weaknesses in the training given. This will help modifications to be made to redress any deficiencies, thus helping future candidates.

The essence of PTS development lies in self-evaluation and making changes to bring about improvement. At the end of any training encounter we need to take stock of what has happened, where we are now and where we go from here.

As a training establishment/trainer, how well have you:

- identified the training needs of your trainees?
- provided an environment where training has taken place?
- planned and designed the training given?
- adapted the training to suit the individual needs of each trainee?
- used role play in the training function?
- delivered the training?
- evaluated the training results?

Only by answering the above questions honestly will you be able to decide what changes need to be made to improve the quality of the training you or your organisation is giving.

Conclusion

Being able to drive is a great 'leveller'. Driving is something which people can do well, if they are taught properly, regardless of their social and educational background. In fact, some people with deprived backgrounds will make much better drivers than others from backgrounds which, in other fields of activity, would be thought of as advantageous.

Most people want to succeed in life generally, and in specific areas of challenge such as satisfying their curiosity and performing tasks well. Driving well gives most people a feeling of accomplishment.

Recent psychological thinking is that ability is largely acquired and that children and young adults can become more or less 'intelligent' according to the family background and support they have and the educational experiences they encounter along the way.

The teacher of driving, therefore, has an immensely important role to play in 'developing people'. It may be that a really good driving instructor could be the best 'teacher' that the learner has been exposed to since the start of their educational journey.

A driving instructor who really knows what he is doing, and is able to offer a sympathetic approach and good motivational support, can often help his learners to overcome the adverse effects of an unfortunate start to their lifetime of learning.

Once they have learnt to drive, these types of learners, receiving the tremendous boost to their confidence, greater mobility and skills useful to many employers which driving gives them, can sometimes go on to much greater things. It can give them a new start in life.

To say that the good driving instructor can totally change the lives of his pupils is no exaggeration.

With the introduction of a separate written theory test for learner drivers which includes questions designed to introduce a 'defensive attitude', there exists the possibility of seeing a reduction in the large number of accidents involving newly qualified drivers. The driving instructor has an important role to play in adequately preparing pupils for this aspect of the driving test and he will have to ensure that his courses cover the syllabus for learners contained in *Your Driving Test*.

Having worked hard at improving the PTS contained in this book which apply best to his particular needs, the driving instructor should have been able to improve dramatically the way in which he brings about learning for his pupils

There is no substitute for good training and practising the techniques covered in this book with real learners. The best way to learn how to drive is to drive, and the best way to learn how to teach somebody how to drive is to teach somebody how to drive.

No two instructors are the same. Personalities will vary from instructor to instructor and no one person can hope to possess all the most desirable traits. As there is no such thing as a perfect driver, there is probably no such thing as a perfect teacher, but this should not stop the instructor who genuinely wants to be the best, striving for perfection.

Continuous self-assessment is the only way forward and each reader of this book will need to work at improving weaknesses and building on strengths. Never forget that technical deficiencies can usually be compensated for by warmth, friendliness and enthusiasm!

The authors of this book wish any instructor who is prepared to accept the challenge and take the trouble GOOD LUCK!

JOHN MILLER   TONY SCRIVEN   MARGARET STACEY

Index

THE DRIVING INSTRUCTOR'S HANDBOOK 1996

'Embraces the wide range of knowledge and skills required to be a professional instructor' **Police Review**

'Is undoubtably essential reading for anyone studying for the Approved Driving Instructor Qualifying Examination and is recommended' **Road Law**

'Makes excellent reading for those in the business of instructor training' **Driving Instructor**

'A great deal of driving sense' **Transport Training**

Whether you are an experienced driving instructor or are training for the Approved Driving Instructor Examination, the new edition of the bestselling *Driving Instructor's Handbook* is the most important investment you could make.

Fully revised and updated, the **Driving Instructor's Handbook** is recommended by the Department of Transport for those studying for the Approved Driving Instructor Qualifying Examination.

The Driving Instructor's Handbook is:

- an invaluable source of reference and information if you are an experienced instructor
- an excellent training manual if you are a new instructor
- a practical aid for everybody involved in HGV, PSV and traffic education
- a guide to professional driving school operation

Widely recognised as the reference source for all trainee and experienced instructors, and for those involved in LGV, PCV and traffic education, the 1996 edition covers all the latest developments, including training and testing of the forthcoming theory 'L' test, the Pass Plus scheme and changes in road traffic legislation.

The current examination and training procedure for trainee instructors is covered in detail, along with the regulations for the ADI register. This includes the upgraded ADI check testing system - essential in maintaining high standards of driving tuition.

£14.99 Paperback ISBN 0 7494 1925 3 384 pages Order ref: KS925
Kogan Page, 120 Pentonville Road, London N1 9JN Tel: 0171 278 0433 Fax: 0171 837 6348

 KOGAN PAGE